Welcome

When you plant a garden you grow more than food and flowers. You create a place where memories are made, emotions are tamed, moods are lifted and inspiration occurs. In this book you'll follow the path of Jim Beard as he grows not only landscapes, but people through gardening, landscape construction and more.

His passion inspires students, colleagues and others to make a difference in their own lives and others. I have been lucky enough to witness just a bit of this first hand.

As you experience Jim's journey of growing people you are sure to be inspired. You will look for new ways to share your passion and special talents with others. And as a gardener, new or experienced, you will appreciate the Do-It-Yourself suggestions for creating raised gardens and growing organic lawns and gardens. There is truly something, actually many things, for everyone who reads this book.

Enjoy!

Melinda Myers
melindamyers.com

Melinda Myers

Gardening expert, TV/radio host and author

Growing People:

How green landscapes and garden spaces can change lives

© 2015, James S. Beard, ASLA, AOLCP and Christopher Jossart, MA
PageTurner Publishing, LLC, Appleton, Wisconsin
www.mypageturner.com

ISBN: 978-1-4951-6094-3

Front-Cover Portrayals ~ design [1]; photos (left): one of four handcrafted pergolas constructed at Brewster Village, Appleton, Wisconsin [2]; (center): Hartling Family Rose Garden, Fox Valley Technical College, Appleton, Wisconsin [3]; (right): 9/11 Memorial dedication, Greenville Fire Department, Greenville, Wisconsin, 2012 [4]

Back-Cover Portrayals ~ design [5]; photo of Brewster Village residents, staff, and volunteers, along with Jim Beard and FVTC students [6]

Proudly printed by Reindl Printing in Merrill, Wisconsin

"When you give, you stop working."

This read is a gateway to understanding how everyday people can find happiness through tinkering in the world of horticulture and landscape construction.

The marks we make in life from playing in soil and assembling growing systems bring livelihood to someone or something, somewhere. You, too, can grow a person or enhance an establishment full of already incredible people… and along the way someone may stop and ask,

"How does this all work?"

Enjoy the stories of growing lives and the simplicity behind a few green structures that you can do yourself! Maybe you'll even pass your time and talents on to someone else.

Find your passion and share it—then you'll never work a day in your life.

Jim Beard

In spring of 2015, the Horticulture Club at Fox Valley Technical College dedicated a young Valley Forge American elm tree to Jim Beard in recognition of his exemplary instruction. One of the students, Donna, brought her daughter, Penelope, to join Jim on this momentous day. Growing people. [7]

Growing
People

How green landscapes and garden spaces can change lives

Jim Beard asked me to write his book with him.

I accepted the request with honor and enjoyed the humbling experience of this collaboration. Thanks, Jim, for the memories and for being like a father figure to me.

Christopher Jossart

Contents

Dedication

This book is dedicated to all the *graduates* and *students* of the Horticulture Technician program at Fox Valley Technical College.

Their passion and perseverance are irreplaceable, and the lives they've touched take my breath away.

All of you have created a legacy in the world of growing people.

Thank you for being an integral part of my life.

Jim Beard

Accolades

A special thanks to the following individuals for putting me in a position to grow lives:

Jerry Eyler, for handing me the keys to build both an educational program and lifelong relationships so as many people as possible can benefit from our work. Thanks, Jerry.

Susan May, for her ongoing leadership and support from day one at the college. Forever grateful, Susan.

Jerry Rickman, for his guidance as both a friend and a colleague during many defining moments. Appreciated, Jerry.

Sandi, my bread and butter in life who keeps me grounded with her gentleness and humor. My love to you, Sandi.

Jim Beard

Preface

A Crowd Grower

It happened a few years ago. In walks this gentleman with a bear of handshake explaining how he had been using worm castings for quite some time in various horticulture studies, and that I was the 'new kid on the block' as product specialist for IntelliGrowth Industries in Appleton, Wisconsin. Jim welcomed me to visit him at nearby Fox Valley Technical College's (FVTC) main campus in Appleton. We talked a short time about his work at the college, its proximity to where I worked, and how quickly I could get to campus for that visit. That was the beginning.

Jim Beard is an impressive individual. As revealed in the preceding paragraph during our initial conversation, notice how his focus was on my needs—even though he didn't really know me. Yes, this was just the beginning. Once I dove into Jim's world a bit by taking him up on that offer to visit Fox Valley Tech, his knowledge, craftsmanship, and leadership came out into the open.

Jim's skills are extensive because there's a story behind every one of his landscape and green thumb projects. One would need a museum to capture the number of projects he's done over nearly 40 years of building really great stuff in so many communities— many of which have been completed on his own time and often with his own materials. In fact, I learn something new from him and about his qualities as a giving individual on a regular basis.

Speaking of learning about Jim and his projects of personal volition, I discovered through casual conversation with some of his colleagues that he volunteered to do a significant landscape makeover a few years ago for an upscale botanical center on Wisconsin's lakeshore. The company decided to give Jim a surprise check as kind of a stipend-type "thank you." Grateful, with that bear handshake of his humbled to a gentle grip, he accepted the check and immediately brought it to the FVTC Foundation to go toward student scholarships. That's just the kind of person Jim is… someone or some group will receive his gifts at any given time. He's a guy who makes his rounds in life to give.

Jim's knowledge of tools, green building materials, and landscape construction and design define a level of craftsmanship that toils in detail. One of his latest projects just before writing this Preface was supposed to be a simple one-cubic-foot box used to measure precisely one cubic foot of material for projects. The detail in the design of this little box was so stellar that it almost felt disrespectful to use it for intended purposes. You'd rather just look at it and get lost in the detail.

Knowledge and leadership pass through to students at Fox Valley Tech thanks to Jim's devotion to learning as a lifelong skill. His students' work on major undertakings for the community come with expectations that, quite frankly, resemble and would sometimes exceed craftsmanship seen on behalf of companies in this industry.

I've had the privilege to attend many of his classes and see the work that is being done. Complete landscape layouts, use of industry tools and machinery, concoctions for liquid organic fertilizers, compost mixes, and greenhouse and hoop house experiments that have drawn national attention— yes, that's what one of Jim Beard's classrooms can look like at any given time. Oh, and more times than not his classrooms aren't characterized by rows of desks and marker boards—they're in woods, fields, or wood sheds, under pergolas, inside a school courtyard, on a curbside. They are everywhere.

What's particularly uplifting about Jim Beard is working alongside of him. We've done presentations and workshops together and shared classrooms. He is a crowd grower. No matter what Jim is talking about, he has an increased following of fans. People turn heads at his gestures that display a passion for his profession. Pens and notebooks are in motion while Jim's knowledge spills out another tip, another tool, and another idea for those in attendance.

> **Pens and notebooks are in motion while Jim's knowledge spills out another tip, another tool, and another idea for those in attendance.**

In a workshop we did together for a rural community comprised of members from several master gardener chapters, the response was thunderous. Beyond a loud clapping that closed the workshop, a gentleman from one of the master gardener chapters said with a hushed voice, "This is the best workshop I've ever been at." He was particularly fascinated by Jim's segment on compost tea brewing, home-built garden spaces, and one of his specialties—raised garden bed systems. These are just some of the concepts you'll be reading about in *Growing People: How green landscapes and garden spaces can change lives.*

Seeing Jim in action connect to a variety of audiences is as much informative as it is entertaining. It's not hard to understand why people gravitate to him. He provides lectures to so many societies, clubs, organizations, charities, and more. Some people I swear just want to attend these functions to laugh. The bottom line... Jim makes you feel at home when he presents. You instantly are welcomed to an arena of friendship. Jim builds your confidence simply by showing that you have an ability to make green growing spaces and related structural components for virtually any lifestyle. Jim's passion is persuasively positive that it drives a yearning desire to go and tinker in soil and structure. He's even been known to toss a few bags of worm castings to attendees at his workshops. The perils of an exploding bag make his events all the more fun.

In a world of sophisticated technology, Jim Beard is his own brand of innovation. He looks at things with an uncanny eye for detail and one goal in mind: designing improvement—something better for those who will enjoy the fruits of his labor and/ or tutelage. That core objective can relate to either something new or an existing concept—like an arbor. Sometimes Jim will use a napkin or even a piece of wood to configure an idea, and he does so with a flair for the Frank Lloyd Wright era of design. He perseveres in this methodology until a project becomes real "on paper." It's kind of interesting how he combines a bit of old school methodology with the latest in green landscape practices to create originality.

One summer afternoon I joined Jim in his backyard for a little peace and camaraderie. I admired a chair on his deck. Its design reflected that from the later Bauhaus era, which originated in 1919 as a cultural movement to combine fine art with industry. Designs from that era are still held in high standards today regarding several elements of craftsmanship.

There were four of these chairs on Jim's deck. They were exact in detail and workmanship. Once again, no surprise; he had built them and several more from a set of jigs he designed to build all the pieces in multiples. Jim was so matter-of-fact about this subject that it was as if we were talking common knowledge.

From that same deck in Jim's backyard I could see a meticulous garden laid out with raised boxes of varying sizes, but again, all of them were placed in precise alignment with attention to detail and comfort for gardening. Objects of his designs reflect Jim's instructional exceptionalism at FVTC. His home mirrors his work—trellises, bird houses, and simple-to-complex arbors. He lives for the implementation of structures that infuse contentment and a sense of home. Jim's mind is always swimming and his work is his passion. When you think of the saying in reference to someone who "walks the talk," Jim is strides ahead of us in ingenuity and sincerity.

I am always at home around Jim Beard, and it is a privilege to be a part of this literary project. Enjoy the many ideas this book will provide you with, and moreover, the craftsmanship and design that goes into his work. Remember, Jim's work tells a story, and there are plenty of life-changing accounts in here as well. I have learned a lot from Jim and you will too in these pages.

Thank you for this opportunity.

Steve Finley, Friend
Chief Operating Officer, IntelliGrowth Industries
Appleton, Wisconsin

Introduction

Welcome Home

A favorite home-away-from-home stop with made-from-scratch goodness is the West Wisconsin Diner in Appleton, Wisconsin. It's a great place to kick back and breathe for a bit, and the menu is loaded with smiles and positive attitudes. The food isn't bad, either, but for Jim Beard—he's lucky to finish an entree because of the people there… regulars, newcomers, and of course, the welcoming staff. There's just not enough time to balance conversation with eating!

The diner is noticeably a regular stop for soldiers of all ages who are home from duty. "Home" for our nation's veterans means something universal to Jim. He served in the U.S. Army for about four years with duties in Korea, Japan, and Vietnam in the late 1960s. Jim was grateful to come home to American soil after his duty was completed. He mentioned that it's a gift to see others enjoy freedom. That understanding is what inspired Jim to complete his mission and return home. Now, he is taking freedom to new heights by inspiring people to grow as individuals through discovering their own sense of expression via landscape construction.

The exchanged pleasantries between these brave soldiers at the diner exemplify one of the reasons the establishment protrudes a homelike culture. If a veteran passes Jim's way there (or anywhere for that matter), he automatically says, "Welcome home, brother" (or just 'welcome home' to a female soldier) as the two parties make eye contact.

Simple exchanges with fellow veterans make Jim reflect now and again. Those moments serve as reminders that his daily travels are only possible because of those who have traveled before him. They empower Jim to live a life that is driven by relationship-building. There is no Rolodex® large enough to hold the number of people who represent Jim's relationships.

Human relationships are the single most critical element in growing people, especially during times of technological dominance. As soft skills fall off the grid of interpersonal communication and text messages perceivably are vying for the way in which job interviews should be done, people like Jim are still shaking hands. The best Facebook® posts or tweets in the universe are no match for the value that face-to-face relationship building brings to life, and Jim Beard is one of the masters. He makes people feel at home with themselves and connects them to success.

Homes-Away-From-Home

Over the past five years alone, more than 100 students from Fox Valley Technical College (FVTC), Wisconsin's largest two-year higher educational institution based on total number of individuals served, have created some exemplary landscape structures for several organizations. Many of these efforts have innovatively found their way into curriculum as hands-on learning experiences, while others simply showcase above-and-beyond deeds. Either way, anytime hands-on learning is combined with going an extra mile—the results are often stellar.

Ironically, several of these structures have emerged as attractions—almost like tourist stops if you will around a pretty good chunk of northeast

Wisconsin. Horticulture Technician students at FVTC have been and continue to be involved in a number of these "landmarks." Their heart and soul has gone into them as demonstrated by media attention, community volunteers who have come out of the woodwork to join in on the projects, and by area businesses that have supported the work.

It's not like anyone could just flip a switch and wham… we have a landscape structure in place! Before any student could lay stone and dive into detail, they had to shake a few hands and grow as a person by working side by side with the very people who represented these partnering organizations. The students were enhancing the homes of other people—whether it be a human service agency, a skilled-nursing care facility, or "home" to whatever product, service, or mission a given business lives and breathes.

You will learn about a sampling of related projects and how Jim Beard and his students made their mark on someone else's home in Growing People: How green landscapes and garden spaces can change lives. It could be at a YMCA regarding a retaining wall project or at a rural fire department with respect to the landscape design and development of a 911 Memorial. Think of all the people your local YMCA impacts every day and all the lives touched by a catastrophic event like September 11, 2001. Home is not just an infrastructure; it's also a state of mind.

Jim's students not only cultivated lifetime relationships with others who were involved in these types of projects; they also realized more about themselves from the experiences. Some took on a greater awareness about community needs; others learned to reflect. Everyone found inner peace through service. In other words, students found homes-away-from home wherever their travels took them, and each student discovered more about him or herself.

What does "home" mean to you?

Home-At-Heart

This book is all about purpose and achievement by way of growing as a person. There are many do-it-yourself books on landscape construction and gardening, and they're all noble. Here we combine some do-it-yourself concepts with a little narrative on the stuff one person and his entourage of green thumbers did along the way to change lives. Jim Beard is the Director of Detail and a pretty darn good storyteller as well. Within each of his stories is another story.

Home is not just an infrastructure; it's also a state of mind.

Jim Beard's passion on the surface appears to be landscape construction. He does not, however, stop at the crossroads of task and another blueprint. His road continues on to the next community, the next organization, the next heart. It's a simple formula for giving that adds a whole lot of purpose into the lives of others. Yes, Jim is expected to teach and mentor as part of his profession. Conversely, to what extent is the tutelage of that expertise shared? Well, there is no limit to Jim's guidance; he just simply recycles doing what's right.

Paying it forward? That's a sincere intention and a catchy phrase made somewhat famous by the 2000 motion picture, Pay it Forward (Warner Brothers, adapted from the book of the same name by Catherine Ryan Hyde). Paying it forward is still heard often around water coolers as philanthropic discussion. We pray the concept doesn't become too rhetorical or that society runs out of resources to "pay anything forward" while good people struggle to make ends meet in a big government era.

Here's food for thought: How about paying it now? It's free—other than your time. So next time you play with your green thumb on, invite someone else along for the ride and teach them a few things. You'll find purpose, enjoy a few laughs, and build a relationship or two. Why wait?

You'll notice at the heart of Jim's ability to grow people is a straightforward plan to train-the-trainer. While he leads and guides, others absorb and tailor. While he communicates, others shake hands and begin to lead. In this book, we refer to "trainees" of Jim's instruction and mentorship as **green baton passers.** The learned pass the baton to learners and the cycle repeats itself, indefinitely.

For the do-it-yourself gardener or tinkerer of design and construction, yes, there's a place in this book for you as well. Beds, Bales, Buckets, and Brews opens up a galaxy of opportunity for any green-thumb enthusiast to experiment with a variety of raised garden beds, "soil less" growing techniques, and at-home compost tea brewing systems (for plant consumption only). Jim provides guidance and leaves the door open for you to build to your liking.

A healthy supply of visuals and renderings culminate the read in a final unit. Jim's objective is to show how the same place where you sleep and put your feet up can easily be a separate, yet complementary, little getaway vacation space as well. You won't even think of a project like this as work, even if you're not completely into landscaping or landscape design—the beauty is found in your personal touch.

Landscape architecture is all about detail. This book's do-it-yourself unit gives you a sense of entrepreneurship by designing and constructing a custom backyard oasis. While reading you may say to yourself, "I can build that." Detail can come in forms of simplicity and personal choice.

Jim's good friend, Steve Brockman, a fellow U.S. military serviceman and recent graduate of the

Horticulture Technician program at FVTC at the young age of 56 after being displaced from the workforce, puts Jim's impact on others in perspective. "Everything Jim does is for the betterment of others," he notes. "I was never on the Dean's List in my life until I came to Fox Valley Tech, and it was because of Jim's drive toward building my confidence that helped me reach this accomplishment. Returning to school after 30 years was not easy; yet Jim made it more than doable—in fact, it was time well spent."

The learned pass the baton to learners and the cycle repeats itself, indefinitely.

One of the reasons Steve believes his time at FVTC was pertinent is because of the opportunities he and others had to work on useful projects. Steve was part of a three-member student team that erected a shed to assist the Horticulture program's growing need to store equipment. He also led a venture to install specialized flooring to align with the program's sustainable greenhouse, which was built thanks to a grant from the Lowe's Foundation. The structure is designed to heat the floor of a greenhouse year round through natural heating.

Steve's many years of work experience were recognized by Jim and put into use for younger students to benefit from. "Jim's always open to new ideas," adds Steve. "That doesn't mean he'll always take new ideas on, but if they can help teach students something new—he's the first one to implement them."

Steve is an example of a fair share of displaced workers who had turned to the college as a result of the economic collapse in 2008. For Steve, he was one of a good number of people looking for either a new skill or a new beginning by way of the Horticulture program. "We immediately felt at home in the program and at the college because of the staff," concludes Steve.

Welcome Home, fellow readers, and enjoy both the stories and green serenity that await you!

Growing People

The world of green landscapes and garden spaces puts us in exceptional positions to change lives, including yours.

1 People, Places, and Swings

A playground project that started in Green Bay spanned to other states and set the stage for years of growing joy.

We've all heard the expression and even said at times ourselves, "I've been around the block." Maybe we've even heard this saying in a third-party context like, "He's (she's) been around the block." In any case, the old proverb is rather complimentary when it comes to referencing some level of a person's life experience.

Any soldier, for example, has been around the block, and any person who has fulfilled a long career has also earned this natural tag of respect. Tremendous wisdom is gained from "being around the block." Why not share those street smarts with others who could benefit from lessons learned by traveling around a block or two? The influence we bestow on young learners, for instance, can take them to places not found in a textbook, heard in a lecture, or seen on a reality TV show.

Block walkers can dutifully show others how to find a block or two themselves. Doing so will only better people. The blocks of Jim Beard's generation are much different than those of today. The impersonal content of social media and the deceit of traditional media are two examples of litter found

on today's blocks. They deceive people away from finding guidance when it comes to building lifelong interpersonal relationships.

Memo: Schedule an hour for a cup of coffee with Jim Beard. His accounts of growing people for more than 40 years will make you yearn for days of yesteryear when handshakes meant more than tweets. We can't return to the past, but we can learn from the relational value it brought us.

Sadly, personal responsibility and a focus on developing interpersonal skills are sliding off the societal grid. They're not as much of a core expectation anymore within a person's upbringing. It's becoming harder to find humility in people while priorities center on self. Jim's model for growing people is an X-factor against these downfalls.

The good news is found within Jim's underlying goal of this book. He simply wants to spark ideas in people who are in positions to grow others—it's just perhaps that they don't see the opportunities. For Jim, he has used landscape design and construction as his X-factor to change lives on a regular basis. He believes we all possess an X-factor to do the same.

Ironically, X-factors are something dear to me when teaching and training both corporations and individuals. [8] The concept deals with finding something in life that distinguishes you from others—yet, in a positive sense, not narcissistic. For example, a basketball player who specializes in rebounding understands the critical role that this skill plays for the betterment of his team. He is not concerned about earning the limelight like those who score points naturally do (not their fault); he is there to do something that offsets him from anything else. A school counselor who uses humor to begin lunch and learn sessions at a college for the community uses the X-factor of making people laugh to help them feel comfortable for ice-breaking purposes.

Notice how there is no ego with an X-factor. Conversely, it's about sacrifice and giving. Jim gives by way of sharing his skills with others. He asked me to write his book with him because he admits to not being a writer. I, in turn, learned that a 2 by 4 piece of wood is not really 2 inches by 4 inches. Admittedly, I am not a landscape construction pro or even an amateur for that matter. People who shine from within do not need a spotlight. That's Jim Beard. He wants his students and the organizations he serves to shine.

As recent founder and trainer of Passion Building™ for both corporations and people, I can appreciate the importance of an exchange I had with Jim during the development of *Growing People: How green landscapes and growing spaces can change lives.* [9] While joining Jim for lunch at West Wisconsin Diner in Appleton, Wisconsin, he struck up a conversation with a couple near the register while we paid the bill. One of the individuals asked Jim what he did for a living. Jim modestly replied, "I work for you." He then expounded on that reply by discussing his role as a horticulture instructor at Fox Valley Technical College (FVTC). His first response to the question related to FVTC being supported, in large part, by local taxpayer dollars. It was a cool experience to hear this reply, and he's right about who he works for!

Jim at times also responds to that same question of what he does for a living as follows: "Before my students grow plants, I grow them as people." Think about how you reply to the same type of question. Notice the passion in his response. Rather than proclaiming a formal title like horticulture instructor, Jim gets to the root of what he really does. That's called passion—a subject matter in which I train to help people move the needle in their lives from getting by to getting ahead, personally and professionally and in the context of finding purpose in life. How cool is it to do something for others and actually see it play out in another person who's already at that level.

There is nothing wrong with using formal titles in response to being asked what you do for a living—eventually, we would all come to that same level of formality anyway in related conversations. The point is… many of us can live with more passion and purpose. If you do, it will show in genuine fashion and not just be some catchy phrase. For Jim, living with passion and purpose goes back more than four decades in an everyday neighborhood in Green Bay.

Jim has walked around a few blocks in his life, and literally, this opening chapter is a portrayal of just that. Blocks of homes and schools formed neighborhoods that became home to playgrounds. We may take the existence of playgrounds for granted today. At one time they were not as commonplace around neighborhood "blocks" as they are today.

It is Jim's pleasure to set a path for growing people by way of a once-upon-time story. That story is about one of the original birthplaces of organic playgrounds in Wisconsin.

A Movement of People and Places Swings into Action

Ever notice an empty park swing moving gently in the breeze? How many times have we seen this image? It's sometimes viewed as a depiction of empty childhoods or even missing children. Regardless of what your first impression is of this image, I think we can all agree that it is one of loneliness and kids.

Jim recalls a momentous moment in the mid-1970s that dealt with an image of an empty park swing. Empty park swings have always touched his heart. After returning from serving for the United States Army in Vietnam, Jim worked as a landscape architect for a firm in Green Bay. His daily travels one day landed him at a meeting on Doty Street on Green Bay's east side.

After the meeting, Jim met some folks who commented on the lack of playgrounds in the neighborhood. The playgrounds that were in place had become dilapidated or hazardous over the years. He also learned that the families in this neighborhood had to cross very busy streets to connect with their kids. There simply was no room for youngsters to play.

It was time for Jim Beard to take a walk around the block, literally and figuratively.

Jim didn't pay too much attention as to why the city didn't have enough playgrounds or why they weren't kept up; rather, he looked forward to a solution. He was called to do something on his own time for children and families. Here was a chance to bring people together, have some fun, learn fresh perspectives, and make something. With an affinity for designing and building things, this project was right up his alley!

Working in collaboration with City officials to make sure codes were met and to rezone an empty piece of land for a playground, along with a few volunteers from the Midtown East Citizens Association (MECA), Jim began a grass roots movement in an everyday residential neighborhood.

On one fall Saturday on an empty parcel of land between two houses on Green Bay's east side, the recipe for growing people commenced. Jim rounded up a few volunteers ahead of time for the project, which turned out to be the installation team of what became known as the development of a **play pocket**. The recreational concepts included the recycling of

tires for swings and railroad beams for structural supports (like a swing set) and bordering (for a play pocket's perimeter), along with the addition of flowers and shrubs for beautification.

Other materials that Jim and the volunteers used were timbers, telephone poles, and stone objects. For that time some 40 years ago, a lot of these materials were considered organic in relation to their intended use—sustainability was now rearing its head in the world of playgrounds. Perhaps the real organic flavor of this effort was found in people. Jim's approach to growing these Saturday morning gatherings from a handful of moms, dads, kids, and teachers to a full-blown legion of volunteers was nothing but natural in its evolution.

The first play pocket germinated into a word-of-mouth "Did you hear what they did over by Howe and Doty" kind of ordeal among neighborhoods. Imagine if texting and instant photography from a phone were around then. Jim would have been building play pockets around the world in no time! Subsequently, as word traveled that these play pockets could be built with minimal or no cost, his volunteer services grew in demand.

Many businesses stepped forward to donate items as well to kind of enhance the look of these play pockets over time. Commercial wood, hardware, and paint were common donations. All of this momentum, according to Jim, would have ceased, however, if it weren't for one key development. He noticed a cultural shift occurring during a time of national unrest with Vietnam and a slumping economy. People **wanted** to do something together that was **good**. Something was "in the air" and all it needed was someone to move it along… a nudge like a gentle breeze.

Recall our earlier reference to a gentle breeze, an empty park swing, and childhood. This time, that "gentle breeze" was blowing toward something full of good in the shape of a community movement.

Jim's instinct suggested this: Instead of asking people if they *could* volunteer on a Saturday morning to put in a play pocket for their neighbored, he would ask them, *"What part of this project would you like to work on?"* The assumption was already in place that people would volunteer, so he directed his energy toward building a network of volunteers that was so succinct that play pockets were done often by mid-afternoon on many Saturdays around town, weather and seasons permitting.

The approach to recruiting volunteers gave people options that fancied their skill level and interests. For example, one person might have carpentry skills, which then created opportunities to lead that part of the project. Another person might like to work with plants or just volunteer his or her time for the exercise by hauling material around. The operation at each site grew in efficiency. It also grew people. Volunteers felt a sense of purpose. The volunteers could leave their personal stamp on whatever part of the play pockets they worked on. Parents who used the play pockets with their kids regularly, for instance, could look up on a beam and say, "It's held in place because we worked on that corner."

Jim took a moment to reflect on those days in Green Bay while we worked on this piece in the book. He did so because something hit him like that empty swing. He was drawing a correlation of those play pocket days to his current role as a horticulture instructor at Fox Valley Technical College and even as a community lecturer. Jim steps away from our chronicling of the play pocket journey for a moment:

> When more and more people give in different ways, things get done in the most natural of methods. It's a very simple equation—allow people an opportunity to do something in which they'll feel

important, and the next thing you know success is realized. No politics, no red tape, no my way or the highway—just a list of tasks with people who are willing to cross them off, one by one.

During the play pocket movement, some volunteers excelled at making connections for donations, by providing food and water, or running errands. These welcomed tasks morphed naturally and complemented the volunteers who were working on building the play pockets with railroad ties, tires, utility poles, and so forth. Jim said that it felt like you were in the middle of what momentum was really like… caught in a moment that's hard to explain unless you were there.

Jim earned the Wisconsin Jaycee's Outstanding Young Man award in 1977 in recognition of starting the play pocket movement.

The features of these play pockets started to evolve even further now. Their look now included tire-climbing structures and bigger swing set units. Over the years into the 1980s, the volunteers grew in number and the forming of task committees offered a bit more organization to the projects. People knew others in neighboring states, like in the Upper Peninsula of Michigan and northern Illinois, and these play pockets found their way across borders.

The whole initiative reached a point where, for instance, one person built horizontal or vertical ladders as his "volunteer job description." He started making these on his own each week in preparation for wherever the next Saturday play pocket build would take place. The movement became a well-organized volunteer force, almost run like a company, and play pockets were all put in on a Saturday in their respective locations.

Throughout the course of the Saturday morning play pocket initiative, Jim changed careers and became a buildings and grounds supervisor for St. Norbert College in nearby De Pere. His new duties introduced other opportunities to serve, but the timing was ripe for a changing of the guard concerning the play pockets anyway. The play pockets had added a relevant component to existing school yards, vacant lots, other playgrounds, and parks.

Many of the play pocket emphasis switched from new construction to maintenance. A consistent maintenance plan was needed for sake of upkeep and safety. Jim and members of MECA, along with some direction from the City of Green Bay, decided to provide guidance for Parent Teacher Organizations (PTO) and essentially turn the project over to them at respective schools (at least around the Green Bay area—it's uncertain what happened at this time elsewhere where play pockets resided).

The PTOs kept up many play pockets for a while; most, if not all of them, however, were completely removed and replaced by modern play "systems" over time. In all, Jim

The Green Bay Education Association presented its annual School Bell award to Jim in 1980 for his design, construction, and supervision of "organic playgrounds" for Green Bay schools.

JAMES S. BEARD
FOR THE DESIGN AND CONSTRUCTION
SUPERVISION OF "ORGANIC PLAYGROUNDS"
FOR GREEN BAY PUBLIC SCHOOLS.
1980
GREEN BAY EDUCATION ASSOCIATION

estimates that about 190 play pockets were built over the course of a decade in three states.

Looking back, people often asked Jim how this movement spread so far and so effectively. In retrospect, notice how many times the word "movement" was used in this story. When egos surrender to a moment, when everyday people laugh at themselves, when one's guard is dropped for experience, and when recognition is replaced by a cheerleader mentality, any task can graduate to a **movement**.

Moreover, Jim stated that the organic-style in which the playgrounds were done in that era was somewhat cutting edge. Simply put, the volunteers were open to doing something that was safer, longer lasting, and more environmentally friendly than the small number of original playgrounds that were in place—all during a time of national unrest. Wow, national unrest? Thank God that Jim is still growing people today while daily headlines scream conflict.

From a publicity standpoint, there was steady weekend TV coverage for part of the first year regarding the play pocket effort back then, but not much more else according to Jim. Had I known Jim then we'd be vying for national media attention on something so meaningful for so many people, no doubt. Humbly and understandably, he spent his time worrying about the progress of the projects for the kids as he naturally would do. The people behind this movement are the story. Bad news sells; good news swells. News coverage aside… this initiative did its fair share of swelling in the shape of changing lives and growing people!

From Parks to Pupils

The playground project era winded down and left behind a tons of smiles, endless pats on backs, and

In 2003, Jim received a Proclamation from the Wisconsin State Senate for volunteer work on 190 playgrounds that began 30 years ago and for a "Garden of Eden" wheelchair-accessible garden at Grancare Nursing Center in Green Bay. The garden included adjoining pathways, raised planters, birdhouses, and a variety of flowers and plants thanks to the efforts of 60 volunteers under his leadership.

success stories under every swing and play set. The volunteers and the support of donors, companies, and City officials sparked inspiration—oh, yes, the purpose of this book in the eyes of Jim.

Jim believed there was now a greater call in his life as a result of the play pocket experience. All the faces, names, places, and so forth eventually became the inspiration behind every blueprint, plant, seminar, and successful student that crossed his path in the form of a new career years later as a horticulture instructor at Fox Valley Technical College (FVTC).

At the young age of 60, Jim's new role seemed like a seamless continuation of what he was doing with that army of good folks around 20-30 years prior. He had enjoyed his time about 30 miles to the north of FVTC for many years working in supervisory maintenance and corporate design, but something was different this time. It was 2004 and new technology greeted fresh opportunities for people in the industry.

Those park days created a later-life chance for Jim to pass his blessings onto others through daily contact with people in positions to grow personally and professionally—perhaps for a career change, a job, to learn or refine a skill, to develop a hobby, etc. That chance created a journey that has led Jim to two outcomes: better lives for people now and greener futures for generations to come.

Sometimes he wonders why it took so long to discover this path on a full-time basis (Jim had taught horticulture in an adjunct capacity at another college for several years). Regardless, as Jim notes, the point is… whether a path finds you or vice versa, we can accept change as a calling. Going through change can be treacherous, but in the end, it can also be a link to fulfillment.

So, there Jim was, in the classroom with a mix of high school grads playing on fancy phones, hard-working people suffering from job loss who were in school for the first time in a long time, and one or two folks trying to find a path to greener

pastures. Everyone there basically had different goals; what he or she wanted to do with a degree in horticulture varied. One thing was certain for all; however, and that was each student's love for plants and green-thumb activities was universally felt.

Jim Beard was on the cusp of showing people how to make a living out of what they know and how to make a life out of what they give. The people Jim touch at FVTC and at his community lectures make others realize that if you find your passion, you'll never work another day in your life.

2 Green Greats

A snapshot of four green structures and their legacy on people

We gravitate to certain people and specific things sometimes without even realizing why. Is there a reason why we select one checkout line over others at a grocery store if they're all the same wait? Is there rationale for why we play golf at a particular course or visit a certain state park basically every time we venture out looking to play nine holes or find serenity? Why do we pick one picnic table or park bench over others to just relax and enjoy a snack or read a book?

Randomness and variety spice up life—true, but deep down we have an eye for what draws us in when it comes to being comfortable in our daily activities. Funny, we don't think of this very often; yet, we wear out the same ole' paths for good reason. Those reasons find us hanging out with positive people and givers, along with being at places of visual appeal.

Take, for example, the aforementioned reference to picnic tables and park benches. We pack up the car for a picnic at a local park in a town we're visiting. We arrive, park the vehicle, and then head for the back of the car to grab the goods. Then what

happens? Everyone scans the park on where to go to enjoy some camaraderie and food, right?

We probably do this kind of thing so often that it's second nature. In this example, what deciding factors are at play concerning where you'll go next from the parking lot into the park? The short answer... what looks aesthetically attractive, right? Granted, attractiveness in any setting is subjective and beauty resides in the eye of the beholder.

That said, there's something special about a place that integrates a little environmental preservation with attractiveness and atmosphere. Those characteristics jump out when you scan those parking lots at parks, rest areas, and so on because they hold an unexplainable identity to them. They welcome you.

Here's some irony. Scanning for that special place to relax and enjoy time with others (or your own downtime) ordinarily doesn't take that long. On the other hand and worthy of a best kept secret, some of these structural places take a fair amount of time to make. How interesting that the eye can catch innovation rather quickly—yet, these types of structures are all about diligently assuring a high level of detail throughout their construction.

So, back to the picnic at the park and decision on where to eat… we often hear "How about over there?" to "That looks nice" to "There's a cool spot," don't we? Without trying much, many of us observe people on campus at Fox Valley Technical College (FVTC) drawn to pergola structures, for instance, due to their warm look and "what's beyond them" feel. A lot of students and employees just go there to get away from it all for a while.

To illustrate the detail behind parking lot moments, we are honored to present four green projects that briefly highlight success at every turn with Jim Beard's landscape construction-related classes representing FVTC. Jim tips his hat to countless industry colleagues who asked, "How much do you need?" in response to a donation request or two along the way to growing organizations, communities, and hundreds of men and women during his time at FVTC.

A precursor is in play pertaining to these four accounts. Jim is employed at a world class organization—Fox Valley Technical College (FVTC) in Appleton, Wisconsin. Jim's word is as good as gold when he says that if you took a little time to see this place, you'd come back… in some capacity—student, trainee, class-taker, or a regular visitor who may hike, bike, or hang out in green tranquility. People should take time to see places right in their own backyard versus hearing about them in the paper or seeing something on television. Some of the most cherished places where we can find healing, joy, peace, and wonder in are right in front of us.

Jim and his students hit a few bumps when designing these staple landmarks, but when it was time to pull out the bolts and drills, their sweat equity forever stands tall in the spectrum of extraordinary achievement. These structures gleam with community spirit and whisper tales of growing people. Enjoy.

Green Roof Rest Station, 2008

Tinkering Leads to an Award-Winning Structure

This little oasis resides on the south side of Fox Valley Technical College's Appleton, Wisconsin campus. It was originally conceived as a rest island for anyone seeking a break during a work day or from a

No one imagined when the Green Roof Rest Station was built that it would earn a Gold Medal from the Wisconsin Landscape Contractors Association for outstanding design and elements of environmental preservation. [10]

The Green Roof Rest Station's colorful upper structure is an immediate draw to the eye. [11]

Students enjoyed learning about the behind-the-scenes details that make the Green Roof Rest Station a structure like no other. [12]

hike along an adjoining walking trail—that kind of intention. Jim was tinkering with some designs and shapes one Sunday afternoon in his woodshop and realized that what we find attractive in life doesn't always have to come with bells and whistles, fancy lights, gimmicks, or glitter. Peace and contentment are today's partners to genuine appeal. Let's use a rest island as a way to inspire the value of downtime, Jim recalls. Electronics, the latest phones, fancy advertisements, and instant gratification feed a fast-paced world; landscape design gives us the downtime to watch it go by.

In season, the colorful roof atop Jim's Green Roof Rest Station (GRRS) resembles a menagerie of brightness and makes you wonder what's underneath. To most of us, rooftops are rooftops. We see them so much they're kind of taken for granted. They are in place to protect a dwelling from moisture and provide runoff, in addition to a capstone of shelter. To that point, roofs are usually shingled with a color scheme to complement a main dwelling's appearance—like a house or building (a lot more options exist today than ever based on green-related materials and other products that catch the eye).

The GRRS's roof structure splashes perennials of beauty to the visitor, yet its design and construction are the real gems behind its existence. A series of partially-concealed angles under each corner add durability to the roof and protect it from high winds and rooftop weight. Jim was inspired by a sustainable roof system on behalf of G-Sky Green Roofs and Walls in Delta, British Columbia.

The perennials are placed in small trays. In late fall, Jim's students remove them from the roof because air can attack roots from all directions. The roots cannot be protected on a roof due to lack of soil and open exposure to freezing, at least where we live! They set the plants, while still in their pans, on the ground and cover them with a light blanket. This way the cold can only attack the flowers from one side, not from four angles.

Sometimes Jim and his students have to start over with new perennials each spring for the GRRS simply because of the process of repositioning them. The station does require a bit more regular maintenance compared to most other related structures. A rubber coating lies between the plant trays and the cedar or fir (either or) wooden part of the roof to delay long-term deterioration.

In addition to its serenity and immediate eye appeal, playful is a good word to describe the Green Roof Rest Station. Jim knew originally that four posts and a box design were needed to frame this type of structure. While finagling a bit with the overall model, he realized the color accentuations atop the roof would lend themselves well to a more playful scheme. Instead of a boxy, tidy appearance, the GRRS morphed into a freer-looking attraction with an original expression of beams overlaying one another. The human eye cannot detect the engineering behind this overlap. This configuration provides a stronger-than-usual support system as well.

The open concept of the GRRS draws a person in and soon the eyes dance around to see how it all works. You know you have something special when at first glance someone wonders how it all works. Large bolts that adjoin and anchor structural sections are often visible in most standard landscape

construction projects. In the GRRS, they are hidden by way of being recessed into six-by-sixes with one-and-a-half inch plugs on each side. It appears the whole station is held together by one-inch and half-inch wooden dowels. The only structural support element that you can see is a quarter-inch cable that runs from one side of the GRRS to the other. It keeps the roof from springing from the weight of heavy snow.

You know you have something special when at first glance someone wonders how it all works.

By using four, six-by-sixes in each corner instead of two (which would suffice in a traditional building sense), the GRRS is actually overbuilt in terms of capacity. Sometimes the visual impact of any given facility is the most important thing when it comes to its purpose. Aesthetics can extend beyond splendor and bring us tranquility. So, if a structure is intentionally overbuilt, then perhaps its purpose stretches beyond just serving as another stand-alone facility to visit. Maybe admiration to detail is all something like this needs to represent.

The GRRS also holds a bit of dichotomy when it comes to strength and durability. Most similar structures place emphasis on holding "up" a structure because of weight issues (snow, mostly in this case). This assembly put elbow grease into holding it "down." Jim and his students' design and construction skills certainly came together to create an edifice that looks like one singular unit without a lot of silos. That is something the students involved in this project are most proud of—in addition to, of course, earning a prestigious Gold Award in Landscape Structures from the Wisconsin Landscape Contractors Association in 2008.

Basically, if wind was to damage this structure, the whole unit would have to lift off as "one unit"—making that likelihood a tall task (unless we're talking about some serious straight line winds or tornadic activity). A 70-mph wind, for instance, would wreak more havoc on the GRRS by lifting it all up in the air like Dorothy's entire home was portrayed in the *Wizard of Oz* (Metro-Goldwyn-Mayer, 1939, adapted from the book by L. Frank Baum) versus part-by-part destruction. Jim's student team went down three-and-a-half feet and poured a six-inch concrete base with an eyebolt cast into the center of it, anchored by rebar and turnbuckles. They virtually created their brand of a "no-fly zone" for the GRRS.

From a drainage perspective, the GRRS originally posed some challenges. As water runs downhill, it's assumptive that your lower level of plants on a roof would drown in this arrangement. To curb this dilemma, the team offset fascia a quarter inch on each eaves trough so the water could run straight down the structure rather than down the pitched roof. The quarter-inch space between two of the pieces of wood on the fascia basically creates an invisible water runoff system. Essentially, the water drips off in confined, consistent areas due to the incorporation of this small space in four pointed areas around the structure.

Even the plants are tailored for this type of growth because of their established root systems. The growing process at FVTC for such plants begins in one of the college's numerous greenhouses or state-of-the art Hydroponics Lab before implementation atop the GRRS roof. Established roots look white, have smaller feeder roots growing off to the side, and are strong in texture. In as little as four weeks, perennials can have an established root system.

Atop the GRRS roof Jim's team laid about 50-60 feet (in proportion to this particular structure's dimensions) of light string or nylon cord right above the soil to help hold plants in place—again, not something visible to the naked eye, but another important detail.

Detail is hard at work and behind the scenes with the Green Roof Rest Station at FVTC, where environmental preservation is found in something gorgeous, warm, and structural. Yes, Jim and his students can marry construction with green schemes for any setting—the community, a backyard, or commercial space. Come see for yourself! Remember though… you might not want to leave.

Riverside Reflection Garden, 2011

A Community Garden Built in a Day

On June 11, 2011, one of central Wisconsin's hot spots for tourism took on another piece of notoriety when more than 80 volunteers, young and old, transformed a 75-by-250-foot piece of land into a place of relaxation.

A dozen Fox Valley Technical College students also took on something new with this project. In addition to conceptualizing, designing, and constructing some of the larger features of this land's makeover from early spring to later that fall in 2011 with finishing details, they led people on a one-day crusade of owning a piece of history.

Citizens from Waupaca, Wisconsin, an exemplary rural city known for its abundant waterways, vast surrounding forests, and small business growth, met early in the morning at ThedaCare's Riverside Medical Center (RMC) to give their health care facility a place of solitude for families, patients, staff members, and the public next to the scenic Crystal River.

The land resided atop a basement foundation of an old physician's building, which was re-purposed over time to serve as an underground storm water runoff treatment system. The surface was ideal for use as something of value for both RMC and the community because it was now just sitting bare as a bit of an eye-sore. Jim's student team was honored to partake, and in some cases, lead the transformation of this parcel into a place of peace where the Crystal River's therapeutic current would complement a calm setting nestled in character. Jim's students thought it was a kick to "take the show on the road" as well to another city a ways from Appleton—about 40 miles. Road trip for these college students!

Jim emphasized how important it was for students to proactively learn as much about any community as possible. They all worked with officials from both the City of Waupaca and the RMC from the get-go to gain invaluable background on the land to formulate a plan. From there, the student team developed goals and ideas for intended usage of what was to become known as the Riverside Reflection Garden. When it was time to collaboratively get the word out about the June 11 volunteer day, the event kind of turned into a challenge of sorts. The partnering organizations derived a fun scheme in good nature wondering if the bulk of landscaping, planting, and supportive construction-related activities could be done in one day. In other words, a good-humored bet was on!

Leading up to volunteer day, the students organized a lot of details to make the event a memorable and positive experience for all. Jim was particularly pleased by how much communication took place by the students while they worked hard to secure some resources and organize donations for a Saturday morning speed build. Come to think of it, Jim recalls, it's almost

The Riverside Reflection Garden overlooks the Crystal River in Waupaca.

A decorative wall project for the Riverside Reflection Garden included a teachable moment with Jim and his students. [13]

Splashes of color and a broad spectrum of green contentment are welcoming sights to visitors of the Riverside Reflection Garden.

Decades of experience working with volunteers has taught Jim one thing: Volunteers will do almost anything if you have roles that are clearly defined for them, or if you give them an opportunity to suggest certain methods in tackling tasks. Here, according to Jim, you're giving them both direction and a voice. Direction is a time saver and credibility-builder toward something that is well organized and purposeful, and a voice provides a springboard to ownership. Growing people, always.

An example of how the students went beyond expectations with this project appeared during the initial phase of the garden's design. RMC staff and administrators were committed to looking at how the new garden would positively impact its culture—in other words, how could patients, staff, visitors, and more use the transformed land? This is an important question to consider. Rather than have that question primarily reside on the shoulders of hospital stakeholders, Jim and his students set out to help define the garden's purpose and value for the organization as a gesture of help.

Jim challenged the students to assist RMC employees in meeting that goal. The green thumb learners went back to the drawing board, so to speak, and made some renderings that highlighted key access points to the Riverside Reflection Garden and spacious sections for patients with mobility challenges. They also created access points to the garden so adjacent businesses and homeowners could enter it from their closest proximity. Then

like the students took over the fun little bet that had been going around with the local folks and Jim. It's like they were preparing to attempt some sort of world record—an adoring little side note that kept their energy and focus piqued.

Prior to that Saturday gathering, the team had the shell, or outline, of the garden defined and most of the gazebos, patios, walls, and path systems in place, but not yet completely finished. The Saturday endeavor focused a lot on planting, landscaping, general labor, and some light construction duties through the use of citizen volunteers.

Another consideration evident in pulling off a community crusade like this that often goes unnoticed in the world of landscape architecture is the behind-the-scenes planning to make best use of volunteers' time (like referenced somewhat in the previous chapter and the play pocket movement).

there were other surrounding elements at play—like how to draw the river into the garden experience, for instance.

This commitment to a methodical approach to understanding the center's use of the garden helped see its completion through in one day. All the preliminary organizational work and pre-analysis kept all the students and volunteers focused on what needed to be done and how those task were to be accomplished. The results took on breathtaking views of precision-like concrete paths and retaining walls lined with wild flowers and green treatments. The plants meander through the garden like a personal tour guide, uncovering accentuations of borderless raised beds and brick patios with comfortable seating. The finished beauty with the river as a backdrop forever whispers sounds of heavy wheelbarrows hauling to and from, shovels tossing dirt, hammers pounding wood, and people laughing while on their knees planting flowers.

A landscaper from Graziano Gardens in nearby Pine River helped choose the foliage for the project—another example of how the community made this a staple landmark for generations to come. The greenery in this setting is deer resistant and full of color and ornamental grasses, with trees and shrubs serving as foundational elements.

Jim recalls one RMC staff member saying to him the following week after that historic Saturday, "You know, this garden immediately became part of us. Looking at it brings the outdoors inside." Jim

took that sentiment to heart and shared it with his students. He believes anyone could package up a comment like that and use it in any community as a template for success.

Jim and the students involved in the Riverside Reflection Garden extend a special THANK YOU to Shelly Christie, John Edlebeck, the entire staff at RMC, Waupaca County Master Gardeners, and Waupaca Public Works employees, in addition to all the volunteers who pitched in to not only make a landmark, but lasting memories as well.

9/11 Memorial, 2012

They Stop to Remember

We were all "there." An intermittent light wind reminded us how close we were to courage. It was the only movement of anything around the large

Jim and his student crew laid the groundwork to what would became a monumental remembrance of courage at the 9/11 Memorial in Greenville, Wisconsin. [14]

Fellow instructor Pat Jensen from FVTC's Electricity program joined Jim for a moment of planning during the initial stages of the 9/11 project. Pat's students also contributed toward the development of the Memorial. [15]

The symbolic pond at the Greenville 9/11 Memorial in its construction phase [16]

gathering. The more than 300 people in attendance were like stone—cemented in prayer and caught in thought about the inescapable. There was no need to call for a moment of silence in the program's script—it just happened on its own.

The horrific tragedy we know as September 11, 2001 made its way in memory on a gorgeous Saturday morning in late August in 2012 in the small, fast-growing village of Greenville, Wisconsin. Its Fire Department hosted a public unveiling of a 9/11 Memorial that featured two real beams that were recovered from each of the two World Trade Center buildings in Manhattan on that fateful day 11 years ago. The aftermath of that vicious attack on U.S. soil brought forth more courage than any medal or frame on the wall could ever signify. That assertion was clearly evident on this day. Jim Beard sat with his head down alongside fellow dignified speakers who honorably were called upon to memorialize this landmark forever on the west side of the Greenville Fire Department.

As a military veteran, a current resident of Greenville, and a Park & Rec Board member, Jim personally didn't have to look far for a reason to get involved in the construction of this Memorial. The small parcel of land devoted to the site came with all kinds of ties to the community, as well as an opportunity to make this place a stop-to-remember respite for travelers heading down Highway 76 or anyone passing through the area.

A 9/11 planning committee in Greenville, which included Jim, Village officials, citizens, and local firefighters, began to visualize how this site would look. There was a relational connection with the Greenville firefighter who courageously fought for lives after the tragedy to a NYFD firefighter in possession of the beams in New York. Jim thought, 'If my students were to be involved in such an endeavor, this one would have major implications.' More on how they became involved in just a bit.

Through the aforementioned relationship between two firefighters, the committee learned during a meeting that two beams from the World Trade Center were going to be transported to Greenville to be part of the Memorial. Amidst the excitement and pure amazement around the room, Jim's mind zoomed into a "kitchen table moment." When the meeting adjourned, Jim instantaneously raced home and began to design. And did he design! With high-tech materials like a pencil and a few napkins in hand, Jim laid down his plan. Fearful of losing a thought, there was no time to dig out graph paper. That came

World class detail by Jim and his students on this paved treasure symbolizes the global presence of the Pentagon. (17)

An amazing lineup of speakers shared a special moment with the community of Greenville during the dedication of the 9/11 Memorial. (18)

The backside of the Twin Tower beam structure at the Greenville 9/11 Memorial [19]

after he recorded those thoughts on napkins.

Jim's "kitchen table moment" produced another dimension to the project's layout. He thought, 'What about rural Pennsylvania and the Pentagon on September 11, 2001?'

The next day Jim cut two pieces of wood to model the Twin Tower beams that had arrived from New York to Greenville (Wow, think about that… from New York to Greenville… never heard that one before! A metropolitan hub with political and commerce implications on the entire world to a small village where the biggest events of the year are Halloween hayrides and youth baseball and softball tournaments—all in a complimentary sense. The transportation of the beams was arranged as the result of a connection between two parties from both municipalities—ones that were about as opposite as bodies of water found in an ocean from those in a backyard bird bath. That didn't matter— the two regions came together in commonality and pure authenticity for a cause unlike any other).

On behalf of the committee, Jim began tinkering with a land-scape outline for the site. The big question at hand was how to project the site in a way that captured the essence of what went down on September 11, 2001. The beams clearly symbolize the

Twin Towers, yet how could other landscape concepts characterize the plane crash locations in rural Pennsylvania and at the Pentagon?

Jim knew that a project like this could easily turn into silos of landmarks, thus diluting the unity of the Memorial as a single structure. Gathering his team together for a big kitchen table moment on site with students proudly donning green Fox Valley Technical College (FVTC) landscape shirts, Jim and his students walked and talked and brainstormed their way to innovation: Rather than prop up the two beams in an isolated part of the property (because they will naturally draw people's attention from basically anywhere in sight anyway), the team devised a layout that would attract the goodness of what the land in rural Pennsylvania and the structure of the Pentagon both stood for before they were destroyed.

The common adage born from this tragedy that was adopted throughout the nation, *Never Forgotten*, encompasses people, loved ones, public safety officials, courage, a nation, and yes, geography. The team's goal was to somehow capture that saying in a visual context.

Consequently, with the beams symbolizing the Twin Towers as the main draw, the idea was to add some simple detail to the Memorial as visitors approach the two structures. In other words, make the path itself pristine in detail. Clean brick was placed in such a way that its elaborate positioning and smoothness contributed toward making a dramatic walk to the Twin Tower beams even more special. The way the surface blends in with green treatments brings a sense of life to both the Memorial overall and a walk toward its main draw. The closer and closer one inches toward these amazing pieces of steel, burnt and bent but not stripped of spirit— they begin to tell a story. This is not something in which you get out of a car and start sprinting at… the two beams consume your heart as you get close to them. It's a walk of memory-making proportions, and some pretty nice elements of detail accompany you along the way.

After gazing at and touching the beams and remembering the pain and utter fear of those who were around these structures in moments of desperation, an impression of tranquility comes over you. The beams are set slightly above a constructed pond. The pond symbolizes the hole in the ground from the crash of United Airlines Flight 93 in rural Pennsylvania. A foreground patio in front of both the pond and Twin Tower beams is shaped to resemble the Pentagon. The beams pull you in; the detailed symbolism of these other 9/11 sites as a whole keeps you there.

Visitors may not notice at first when they approach the Twin Towers at the Greenville 9/11 Memorial because of their fixation on the beams, but the brick walkway mentioned earlier is made up of named bricks of both firefighters and military veterans from Greenville. Furthermore, the beams are positioned in a direction that points right to the fallen Twin Towers in Manhattan… a little side note of geography.

Symbolism is everywhere with this heartfelt project, including the soft light that shines on the main section at night in memory of all who lost their lives on September 11, 2011. Even a tree that sits next to the two-beam structure ushers symbolism. Jim and his students planted a crab apple tree in that spot to symbolize a Callery pear tree. That pear tree became known as the "Survivor Tree" after enduring the 9/11 attacks at the World Trade Center. About a month after the attacks, the tree was discovered at Ground Zero severely damaged, but not destroyed completely. It was removed from the rubble and cared for by the New York City Department of Parks and Recreation. After a miraculous recovery, the tree was returned to Ground Zero where it continues to grow today as an ongoing icon of resiliency, survival, and rebirth.

Like we often observe at FVTC, which is less than five miles away from this site in Greenville, collaboration in the community comes with no conditions or restraints. Welding students from one of the college's Oshkosh training centers made the stainless steel wall at the 9/11 Memorial that reads *Never Forgotten.*

This whole effort fascinatedly started before any discussion of a 9/11 theme surfaced. Based on the positive reputation that Jim and his students earned in Greenville a couple of years prior to this project through a separate endeavor, the Village's Park & Rec Board didn't have to think twice about who to enlist to oversee the Memorial. One of Greenville's strategic objectives for quite some time has been to make the Village more sustainable. Initiatives that put more 'green' in Greenville have moved to the front row of prioritization in recent years.

For example, the Village wanted to install a rain garden at its municipality building (across the street from the fire department where the 9/11 Memorial resides) to highlight sustainable practices and a commitment to green. After receiving a number of bids for the design and construction of a rain garden, members of the Park & Rec Board decided not to move forward with the project due to cost factors. All of the bids simply came in outside of the Village's designated budget for the project.

God puts us in places at certain times for a reason, and in this case, Jim Beard. Ironically, FVTC's Horticulture Technician program happened to be exploring sustainable practices and projects with utmost importance for several reasons, mostly because it's the right thing to do and students need skills in this practicum. Long story, short, horticulture students took on the rain garden project for Greenville and the rest is history in terms of success. The rain garden, located on the west end of the municipality building, is a nice blend of plants and gravel creek beds. It holds about 650 gallons of water before it slowly overflows into a runoff system by serving as a filter from rain atop the roof of the municipality building.

Here's another drum roll… these students built the rain garden with residents from Greenville in ONE DAY. Remember Waupaca? I think Jim hit a niche here in structures that can go up in one day! Granted, a lot of pre-planning, advanced work,

and follow up detailing and maintenance are still required for projects of this magnitude, but yes, the lion's share of the labor is done in one day.

Most importantly, the rain garden results built trust and relationships between the college's program and the Village of Greenville. So, when it was time to explore the feasibility of a 9/11 Memorial, guess who was top of mind to help?

You can see that the process of design, construction, and implementation of Greenville's 9/11 Memorial heavily weighed on symbolism. Incorporating that overall theme into the process of making the Memorial added a fresh twist to learning. Some students were a bit young when this deadly event happened. Subsequently, working on this type of build supplied them with genuine knowledge of something that was never seen before on American soil.

This particular project included a rather emotional and comprehensive program that was instituted to formally unveil the site. Herein was another way students could expand their skills by participating in an event of great significance. Speakers included firefighters, witnesses, and even a retired New York City firefighter who was in the trenches trying to save people. Lieutenant Joe Torrillo had people reaching for handkerchiefs while his sharp New York accent talked about that day in 2001—he knows those beams all too well.

Other speakers included Walter Zerrenner, a Greenville resident who worked in New York during the time of the attacks. He witnessed smoke coming out of the North Tower and the sheer disbelief of one of the world's largest cities shutting down on a dime. Luke Laidley joined the gathering from New York as well on that amazing day to help unveil the 9/11 Memorial. He worked for Morgan Stanley on the 61st floor of the South Tower. Luke felt the building shudder from the impact of United Airlines Flight 175. He worked 16 floors below the crash site and escaped the dark and smoke-filled building. Jim and FVTC President Dr. Susan May were honored to be part of the program as well—Jim as a speaker and Dr. May as a special guest.

It's one thing to read or see a broadcast about dedications or events pertaining to 9/11; it's another thing to be "there." No spin, no sensationalism, no political tie-ins, just pure authenticity from those who wear this on their sleeves. We were all "there" during this program in Greenville.

Jim extends exceptional thanks to the citizens of Greenville, members of the Greenville Village Board and Administration, the Greenville Fire Department, the visitors who joined the dedication from New York and beyond, the attendees, and to all we hold in our hearts as survivors, rescuers, and the deceased—who are the most courageous of all. Here's to you and your families forever in prayer.

And special thanks to the FVTC students straight from Jim. They earned the right to lead the construction of this monumental site thanks to a class before them who set the table with professionalism during the implementation of a rain garden. A couple of students worked on both projects. Their futures will shine a little brighter because of what they will remember, and that being: *Never Forgotten*.

The front view of the Twin Tower beams at the Greenville 9/11 Memorial [20]

Brewster Village, 2014

As Close to Home

"I'll be next door to touch up on that patio we put in last year." "We're heading over with these perennials to play in the soil and see what we can do to the east side of the village." "Those bricks around the south pergola could use a little edging."

The comments above from Horticulture Technician program students at Fox Valley Technical College are unscripted, unplanned, and unequivocally full of passion. There's energy behind these statements from learners as much as there is a yearning to visit what has grown to be a favorite place of theirs. It doesn't matter if the student is fresh out of high school or an older person looking for a career change, or anyone in between—the place is Brewster Village.

Brewster Village is a quaint, cottage-like community that offers short-term rehabilitation, long-term nursing home services, and more. Its residents, aka… villagers, and staff members are the friendliest around, and the organization exudes an upbeat, welcoming culture that Jim and his students have come to adore. Just recently, Brewster Village began to start offering something else for those who call it home… a story-telling view.

Days of wonder and stories of life whisper in colorful flowers that dip and bend in breezes around Brewster Village thanks to a makeover by the students under Jim Beard's direction. A poor attempt at poetry aside in that previous sentence, have you ever wondered what peace felt like? You can while harbored under one of four new pergolas at Brewster, and for its villagers, these homelike sanctuaries deliver a great setting for them to relive peaceful memories. Literally, the shrubbery around the structures kind of captures a person to be at one with himself or herself and nature.

Clean, stone pathways safely take residents to pergolas of contentment as close to home as possible around their gorgeous village—whether they're in the element or viewing it from within the main building. Depending on a person's vantage point of the pergolas, particularly one that is nestled in the northwest corner of the grounds, it's hard to even see if anyone is enjoying the serenity under its top beams. That's because of the partnering plants that have adjoined so close to the structures in creating

Students gathered with Jim to review some of the completed work at Brewster Village, which included planting flowers, trees, and shrubs, putting in stone and brick pathways, and the construction of arbors and pergolas. (21)

intimacy for villagers and their family members.

These elements offer a different look to Jim's community projects to date—the integration of green and wood to manufacture peace. Most of his previous work with students and pergolas utilized plant life to accentuate pathways leading up to them. At Brewster, green life bucks right up against the pergolas that they appear to be "built in" them. The appearance certainly displays a sense of dwelling for sure in that it wouldn't be too far-fetched to want to camp there.

Brewster Village began as a project management learning experience for students to become involved in a full-fledged makeover for an organization. Why? Location and timing. Brewster is the next door neighbor to FVTC's Appleton campus. Located just south of the college's 144-acre campus, the county-run organization is literally a five-minute trail walk through the woods from the college's Service Motor Company Agriculture Center, which houses the Horticulture program and more.

From a timing perspective, Brewster Village opened in 2001 and was ahead of its time. It transformed the skilled-nursing care facility into a community village. Brewster Village now looks like it should be nestled

Elements of shade bring tranquility under one of the custom-built pergolas at Brewster Village. [22]

Growing people runs the gamut at Brewster Village between villagers and their family members, volunteers, employees, and FVTC students. [23]

somewhere alongside a cozy lake—a far cry from its earlier appearance as a rather institutional-looking, square building with not many windows (not to anyone's fault—that was kind of how nursing homes were constructed for a long time). Brewster's look today is a myriad of circular and octagon-like modern "cottages" from the outside. Inside, the rooms and halls are like little communities where villagers can gather in a sundry of amenities and services like you were in a town, complemented by street names and a ton of light from big windows.

As part of Brewster Village's new look, all involved realized they needed to make the most of their external space to run in harmony with a fresh inside design. Understandable. Facility makeovers and commercial construction are the biggest drivers of necessary landscaping. Outdoor elements serve as greater forms of first impressions than ever before, and increased environmental regulations contribute toward the need for landscaping plans as well.

Brewster Village looked to outside contractors for landscaping and related maintenance work, but those arrangements didn't produce satisfactory results. Some staff members heard about what Jim and his program were doing around the community from the media and decided to explore a partnership. The outcome thus far of this new accord has been nothing but cutting-edge.

Talk about the proverbial win/win collaboration. Brewster Village works with FVTC's landscaping and plant maintenance crews on a seasonal basis. The remainder of the year's work is tied directly back into volunteer learning projects aligned with the college's curricula. Brewster Village has evolved into an ongoing outdoor learning lab for landscape construction, horticulture, and plant maintenance studies at FVTC.

The students are over there regularly, and during peak times, they even earn a paycheck as part of the agreement with the facility. It's a real-life set up where students can advance their leadership and technical skills. They are now working as a "real company"

per se, providing services to a "real client"… what a great public/public partnership.

It's rather fascinating when timing meets a logistical opportunity, isn't it? Before Jim became aware of the situation at Brewster Village in terms of its landscaping needs, to no surprise he had considered doing a project or two there purely from the standpoint that the organization was next door. Having an opportunity to do something that benefits older adults in later-life made this project a slam dunk for Jim and his students.

Brewster Village also supplied the college's landscape construction class with a novel concept. Since the location was a hop, skip, and jump away, it was time to raise the bar on developing skills in students. No longer were transportation or geographical concerns as big of an issue for students—and yes, no more excuses associated with said factors. Proximity was now an advantage in regard to project management. Students had extra time to build relationships with staff members and patients by engaging them in the process of what they'd all like to see put in as landscape construction upgrades or additions, as well as plant life.

For these reasons, the Brewster Village project was ideal for advanced skill set development in communications, planning, leadership, teamwork, and more. Plus, with the recent remodeling of the organization from a more institutional look to a cottage theme, another opportunity presented itself in the shape of a clean slate. There was really nothing to go off of from a previous design or green plan at this facility.

None of Jim's Brewster Village landscaping team members were experts in the field of skilled nursing or end-of-life care, but they heard from several folks there about a correlation to health and home. Put another way… one's outlook on life is somewhat dependent upon his or her surroundings. If nursing home residents feel like they're at home, then their state of mental, emotional, and/or physical health can often lead to a better quality of life or even prolonged life in some cases. What do people miss once they have to say goodbye to living independently? One of the top answers… their surroundings.

That's where plants, pergolas, arbors, patios, berms, pathways, and more come into play—they all create surroundings of serenity and beauty. These characteristics draw us to a place called home. They give life. For some, life is all too short at this stage. Jim recalls one of his students, Mason, a 21-year-old from Shawano, Wisconsin, leading a conversation on behalf of other students with some villagers in early summer of 2014. They asked him for a butterfly garden. Mason and other students planted flowers like daisies, milkweed, and cornflowers to attract butterflies.

For Mason, he learned that he has both the freedom and knowledge to make someone else's life better. For some Brewster villagers, they now have new life in their world. Color, new plants, butterflies, and the people behind the fulfillment of a simple request all concocted lifelong relationships, knowledge, and lessons. This is something you can't buy.

Overall, the jewel of the Brewster Village project is a fixture of comfort and privacy for its villagers and family members. They have serene places to congregate and just be together as a family. Jim's team replaced stone slabs that were used as old benches and built pergolas with comfortable seating under them for comfort. At this moment, the college's Horticulture students still maintain Brewster's annual and perennial flower beds, trees and shrubs, and pot vegetables that individual villagers can grow in the facility's courtyards.

As of summer of 2015, Jim's team planted about 8,000 new plants both the year before and during this season at Brewster Village. Some are not immediately adjacent to the cottages—it's all part of a long-range plan of beautification and preservation for the organization, in addition to cultivating relationships.

Those relationships are already in full bloom. In addition to the students' interactions with staff and villagers, one of the most memorable scenes from the project thus far was seeing an 83-year-old man in a motorized wheelchair take this effort under his wing, so to speak. A fellow U.S. military veteran of Jim's who served in the Korean War, Bob Yandre took the project as his special daily task by watching the students and talking with them from the get-go. He was one villager that didn't miss a beat when it came to seeing the initiative go up, step-by-step.

Bob's interest in Jim's students grew in their hearts. He spent 52 hardworking years operating a backhoe in the construction industry, and his passion for building resonated with joy by hanging out with Jim and his students on a regular basis. The team designated him as "Honorary Foreman" in conjunction with a brief ceremony to culminate the completion of the structural part of the project that featured a final arbor going up.

During this little christening session, which drew media attention, Jim invited Bob to be the first person to travel a new walkway at Brewster that led beneath an arbor and into a newly-constructed pergola. As he guided himself through the structures with a smile from ear-to-ear, a large applause ensued with tears.

Thanks, Bob. Thanks, Brewster Village. See you tomorrow.

Green Godsends

The following snippets scratch the surface of how simple it is to build lives through landscape construction and some green thumb projects. They don't have to be on a large scale. Invite people to your backyard, visit a friend or colleague's front yard, volunteer your time to grow lives with hands-on sweat equity, or preserve a green space for future generations.

For now, let's conclude this opening unit with a sampling of sounds that Jim and his students heard throughout the course of the four projects from other students, recipients of their work, and community members in general. Green Godsends grow people…

I stopped and looked at the structure for no particular reason other than to say, "Wow."

I wonder how it all works.

We didn't know they could refine their construction skills to make whatever they want.

This project gives our community something that no other community has.

This area immediately sets the table for what kind of campus you're visiting.

As a student, this project makes you look at doing something until you get it right, and then you realize you can do it all over again a bunch of different ways.

You learn to respect detail and value all ideas.

I've never seen this before.

There is no "almost right" when you make something in this industry. There's a right away and a wrong way. Only by making mistakes will you learn this moment… a moment that hits you between the eyes.

I never knew you could build something like that.

It makes an already fun job even more joyous by seeing such craftsmanship.

You felt like you were there.

You look at something like this and instantly remember.

2

Green Batons

Glimpes of new pros in the green industry passing batons to grow others

3 Pair Tree

A pair of students grew to realize they're in positions to change lives.

Put in Position

Train-the-trainer. Apprenticeship. Job shadow. Hands on.

Call developing the next generation workforce what you want. The important thing is we're calling it something. The process of training another person for a career and a better quality of life is why Jim Beard and most people in his profession get out of bed every day. As noted, Jim considers how he spends his time as not even work. He knows that what he does contains a nugget for the very people he educates: an ability to pass a baton of knowledge onto others.

There is a certain fabric within our calling to teach beyond technical aptitude. In other words, we can open doors to cultivate new relationships for others and set the table for future generations to succeed IF we recognize that mentorship is as positively powerful as instruction. We're in a position to be once-in-a-lifetime mentors to others. Holistic intervention is the name of the game today in the field of education.

Let's put ourselves in the shoes of the learner for a second here… they, too, are in a distinct position. Most students are going to look to someone in a position like Jim's with natural receptiveness purely because they are investing time and money to improve their lives. Wow, what a running start to change a person's life!

Some learners will naturally not reach the level of an instructor in terms of sharing and teaching his or her new knowledge with others, but that doesn't matter when it comes to growing people. A baton pass of knowledge by sharing our time and talent with someone else who could in turn do the same and so on is a hand-off of epic proportions. The model has always been there for us to follow—not sure we've identified or embraced it enough.

"Life is really simple, but we insist on making it complicated." Confucius.

Growing People: How green landscapes and garden spaces can change lives is pure simplicity. The practice of changing a life here and there along the way in doing what we're passionate about is yours for the taking. It depends on how you want to live your life.

The most complicated part of this book for me was learning that a 2 by 4 piece of wood is not really 2 by 4 in its actual measurement. I racked my brain for some time to figure this out (I eventually called Jim to end the pain).

I was raised in a wonderful environment to learn but perhaps was too disinterested in building things that would have introduced me to the measurements of a 2 by 4. My dad built beautiful grandfather clocks as a hobby and would have shown me anytime about wood and dimensions, etc. I just wasn't interested. So, when the 2 by 4 came up in Unit 3 of this book, I found a few hairs on my keyboard from pulling them out in goodhearted frustration. The other part of the book I could relate to; therefore, there is something in here for the teacher in all of us to the green thumb fanatic… to a little bit of both.

The previous unit sheds light on ways that Jim grows people by involving them, start to finish, on planting excursions and landscaping projects. His unification of people through these projects formulated a platform for teaching invaluable life lessons. You don't have to build something big and bold or transform a parking lot into a botanical mall to change lives—you just have to put others in positions to do the following, as one will lead to the other:

- **Self-discover** (something, someone of influence, or themselves)
- Find a **purpose** from that discovery (what something or someone needs)
- Realize that your purpose creates **success** for you and others (everyone grows!)

Perhaps you can take ideas from the projects in this book and modify them or build the concepts to scale, or maybe you will find contentment or even a new skill or two from the readings. Regardless, either you will learn something or someone else will grow as an outcome of these experiences. Green projects bring out the best in people because there is a niche for everyone involved to feel like they have accomplished something.

Incidentally, the buck doesn't stop at any given experience either when it comes to learning and growing people in a green setting. As educators, it is dutiful to build responsible leaders as well as technical experts, and Jim has found the way to do so. It requires a little less hand holding at times while putting learners in positions that render accountability. Let them find their way a bit and let go of your desire to be popular.

Jim is excited to introduce a sampling of success stories in this literary work on behalf of a legion of people who joined him every step of the way. While each class passes before him and another community project hits the rearview mirror in completion, keeping tabs on students, graduates, and colleagues becomes a challenge for him. That challenge is actually what keeps Jim ticking (in addition to all the wonderful folks who ask him to speak regularly about gardening and landscaping).

For example, Jim gives to you Dan and Mason, two recent graduates of the Horticulture Technician program at FVTC. These two gentlemen both bring to life a steamroller effect on growing people in their stories. Dan and Mason each matured in special ways through some hard lessons, and now they're both in positions to pass the green baton.

Paired for One

Anyone who happens to be in the company of Dan and Mason is in a good place. They each epitomize the profile of learners in the program who have such a passion for taking what's in front of them to the next level. Others before them have preceded their exemplary work ethic. This excerpt, Paired for One, is dedicated to those individuals. The flavor of Dan and Mason's work just happens to involve a very special third party—someone who changed Jim's life the day he met him.

Shortly for a while the voice of this book will be turned over to Dan and Mason to bring you up to speed on this new member of the program's learning team. Enjoy how Dan and Mason, who again had to endure their own lessons, became mentors thanks to being put in positions to self-discover, find a purpose, and succeed. They will recount their collective work as mentors to a 22-year-old young man who lives with severe autism.

Some background… the program's new friend came to Jim at Fox Valley Technical College through a series of referrals. His name for sake of this excerpt is fictitious for we will refer to him as Mr. B. The first day Jim met Mr. B. he was humbled all over again through one smile.

Initially, Jim had arranged for Mr. B. to visit the program's Hydroponics Lab three days a week with his caseworker to expose him to small plants, microgreens, and seedlings for about 45 minutes-to-an-hour each time. His parents and caseworker were seeking fresh ideas for him to find greater worth in a personal enrichment activity. Jim and

The Hydroponics Lab at FVTC opened up a world of discovery for Mr. B. (24)

his students were honored to take Mr. B. under their wings. Jim paused right after he disclosed that statement, "Wait, maybe Mr. B. was taking us under his wing," he said with a hint of mystery.

The truth is… Jim would say something like that because he comprehends that this type of opportunity doesn't happen every day, and when it does, there's a reason. Let's simmer the whole "under one's wing" idea for now.

Jim receives referrals sometimes at FVTC that go above and beyond the Horticulture program's ever-changing curriculum—everything from national soil tests to organic studies to the community projects referenced in *Growing People: How green landscapes and garden spaces can change lives*, and more—but never had anything like Mr. B. come his way. The opportunity is both heartfelt and captivating from the standpoint of autism and plants as a combined synergy—a somewhat pioneering form of therapy—at least in this neck of the woods.

There was no set timeline in place for Mr. B.'s arrangement; Jim was going to causally see how this collaboration played out with his students. Mr. B.'s primary team, comprised of Jim, Dan, and Mason, slowly introduced the Hydroponics Lab to him and his caseworker to help determine a feasible plan for his activities in there. The lab set the stage for a quiet, cozy setting for him to discover a lot of green and the soft side to growing gentle plants.

Mr. B. is highly intelligent and a fascinating person through watching his array of expressions and communication styles. He animates a zest for life and a passionate learning style. Do we do that enough in our lives or do we try to be someone we're not? Jim is eager to learn and pass the baton of knowledge himself immediately after hanging out with Mr. B for a short time. "Give me passion over popularity any time," Jim notes. He struck a chord right out of my training sessions to companies and individuals. Thanks, Mr. B. and Jim.

Expectedly, Mr. B. was a bit overwhelmed during his first visit and new venture with green. Oh, that smile, though—he's got the widest and brightest form of happiness in that smile. It attracted others to be around him. Dan and Mason were among the first to gravitate to Mr. B.

These two former students directly remain connected to the college and have a lot of supplemental duties on their plates—Mason is pursuing another degree and working in the industry. Dan too, is working in the industry and taking new courses related to golf maintenance studies. That said, it didn't surprise Jim that both of them kind of "adopted" Mr. B. Let's see how they're passing the green baton.

Dan and Mason share…

DAN: At one time I thought I had all the answers in life. Funny, now I realize I really don't know much at all—except for perhaps more about what matters. That's all because I've met Jim Beard. After a run-in or two with the law and some bouts with substance abuse, I casually heard about a program at Fox Valley Tech that deals with golf course maintenance from my neighbor, Patti, an employee there. Since I'm into golf and nothing else was really happening positively for me at the time I learned about the program, I thought, 'what the heck.'

I met Jim while first taking Horticulture classes toward this degree. I saw him everywhere in the center that houses the classes, along with a huge variety of agriculture offerings and some outdoor engine stuff. Jim's presence is bigger than reality at times—when you see him, you know something

important is going on. Maybe that's what I needed in my life—a purpose, and I guess that is what drew me to him.

When your life is down and out, people can find it easy to judge you. I don't hold that against anyone—it's understandable. I've made a boatload of poor decisions. A natural reaction to a person's troubles is to grapple with why I made poor choices about drugs and related behaviors. This results in theories relative to what type of person "would do such things."

I suppose a person can gain a sense of despair when all he or she hears or suspects is this type of judgment. Consequently, you begin to realize that a drug is your only friend because it knows you better than a person does. Through the grace of God, I quit drugs with a clear understanding: One more shot is all I got, and that chance was now made possible through working with plants.

Jim was the first person in a long time who didn't judge me—he tried to get to know me first and foremost as a person above all else. That special bond with him enabled me to focus on school, not on outside influences. Good grades came my way for the first time ever and the peers around me felt like family. I believed I could do this whole school thing after all. I found my niche with plants, turf, soils, and so forth.

Isn't that part of what life is about… finding a niche? Once you find your niche, it can expand, diversify, or remain as controlled or free as you want it to be. It's also purposeful, but like anything of value in life, it comes with price. What did I pay? A little tough love.

Jim Beard sets robust expectations. He does so knowing that reaching results will do more for a person than basically going through the motions. I didn't want any more going through the motions, lazily waiting for the next unreal thing. Jim's been around the block, and he knows how to set people up for success if they pay a few dues. Drugs were easy but where was the success? Earning good grades and setting and attaining goals were hard, but now I tasted success.

So have countless others in the wake of Jim's company. I can't guess how many times I have seen former students come back to the college and thank Jim for basically anything or everything. Another neighbor of mine, for instance, was one of Jim's former students. Boy, it's a small world—isn't it? Anyway, this acquaintance of mine was hired by a landscaping company before he even finished his courses. Growing people is what Jim does in a nutshell.

Jim reminds me a lot of my grandfather, who was a rock in my life for too short of a time. He never got the chance to see me succeed, so in a way, my triumphs are shared with him spiritually through Jim. I never thought I would experience such a connection like this with ties to a family member.

One day I started an internship for Jim around the campus, working on various landscaping projects and plant experiments. I believe this internship happened for a reason. I remained an intern for a year and a half. Now I was starting to grasp why so many people thank Jim on a regular basis. His knowledge quickly filters into others. If you listen to Jim and practice what he does, only good can come from hanging around this guy. After a short while I absorbed a bunch of industry knowledge from Jim—enough to land me 10 job offers before I even graduated.

What was it then that kept me in that internship for so long? Words like attitude and outlook come to mind. Catching on to what Jim is teaching was a walk in the park since he's such a great instructor; it's how you take that walk in the park and apply the knowledge that's key. Waking up each day with newfound confidence to get my head straight and grow myself as a person for whatever comes my way next in life is now how I live. Jim will always be my life coach… way more than an instructor to me.

Near the end of my internship, I noticed Jim working with a young man and a lady in the Hydroponics Lab. Jim could gage that I was ready for a new challenge that would help me to hit the ground running with a new career which I had accepted in the field of green. Funny… he just knew this was a precursor to my entering the professional world; yet, there was more to this opportunity. What was it?

If you listen to Jim and practice what he does, only good can come from hanging around this guy.

Jim asked if I'd like to take on helping this young man, Mr. B., in kind of a guidance role in exposing him to micro-related growing techniques. Mr. B. was not a student; he entered our program through some referrals within the college as kind of an activity-based set up for his betterment.

This challenge was completely new to me. In the past I would have hesitated repeatedly over something like this. Now, such apprehension was gone in the blink of an eye. Let me tell you how uplifting that feels! No more doubts in this heart—only confidence! When you have confidence and people believe in you—life is a completely different ball game. Plus, going through what I did prior to coming to FVTC is nothing compared to how positive Mr. B. lives his life with challenges resulting from autism. I'm small potatoes next to him. I believe Jim had this in mind as well when asking me to work with Mr. B. Jim wanted me to know humility, and he also wanted me to leave a special mark on this young man.

Gut check time… with confidence comes not only humility, but patience. Patience is necessary to not overlook detail, and it is an essential gateway to lifelong learning. Jim positioned me with Mr. B. for a few reasons, and I was soon to understand a big one in patience. Mr. B. reminded me that life's treasures are found on interpersonal levels.

This courageous man openly expressed his thoughts, and even if you can't interpret them—that's irrelevant. When around him, I could detect one certainty. He really didn't judge me or my fellow program peer, Mason (who you'll hear from in the turn of a few pages). If anything, Mr. B. seemed to understand our roles with him—we were opening up a world of little greens to discover.

How pure—someone without pre-judgmental notions or pre-conceived bias. We can all grow from Mr. B. on these principles alone, don't you think?

Mr. B.'s demeanor floats lightly with calmness and contentment when he is around plants. It's like he's completely consumed in moments so deep around micro-greens at all growth stages that he's like one of them. He goes from openly expressing his persona by kind of dancing around in joy when around these plants. Mason and I planted some peas and beans in the Lab and had Mr. B. follow us around. Soon he started watering them as "his thing to do" during every visit.

Once Mr. B. became more accustomed to his surroundings, Mason and I had him plant red radish microgreens that we grow for the Culinary Arts program at Fox Valley Tech. His gentle touch with plants is remarkable. We started noticing during each visit that Mr. B. began heading toward the greens he planted the previous week to check on their growth. He slowly started taking a mental inventory of his work.

With that in mind, Mason and I implemented a system for Mr. B. where he could harvest last week's microgreens and plant new seeds that will be ready for harvest the following week, or weeks. It was inspiring to watch him comprehended aspects of time with measurement. He built one process on top of another by managing his time between watering, planting, and harvesting. This young man was growing.

Mr. B. loves feeling the soil and its variety of textures. Occasionally, we'll all plant plugs together in flats. Such a task is right up Mr. B.'s alley. He gets to dig in the soil by filling flats and then planting plugs. The sequential undertaking is done methodically and with wonderment. He also at times, under supervision, cuts coleus and geraniums to grow roots off leaves, forming the development of new plants. Mason and I marvel at his precision and patience. If Mr. B.'s doing something with plants, those greens are getting the best service imaginable by way of his acute attention to detail.

Mason (left) and Dan worked regularly with Mr. B. in the Hydroponics Lab, and the three of them grew together as lifetime friends and learned some life lessons from one another along the way.

The three of us made a terrific team and we celebrated together quite often after completing a flat or replanting job. We made trips to the main greenhouse a few hundred feet away from the Lab. His voice comes to almost a hush in there. He loves the scene in the main greenhouse!

Mr. B.'s growth tugs at the heart. From watching—he started doing, and from doing—he started taking on more. From once following—he started releasing trust in us and building confidence in himself. Mr. B. advanced himself to a point where he productively tinkers with plants on his own. Mason and I have grown right with him; he has taught us new ways to look at detail, patience, and to make the most of any moment. Who knows… the three of us could turn into the green version of The Three Musketeers! I'm going to make sure Mr. B. is always a part of my life—somehow, some way, as I begin a new professional journey. Thanks, friend.

MASON: The general studies coursework at a four-year university wasn't doing anything but slipping me deeper into uncertainty. Nothing against that pathway—it just wasn't my ticket. I needed to wrap my head around something tangible… visible, hands-on. While fumbling around on the web looking for a new academic direction, the word "horticulture" hit me for some reason. I knew the concept had to do with plants, which have always fascinated me; yet, there was something more beyond this term… an element of mystery.

For starters, I guess I never drew a sharp connection between plants and a career. Curious enough to find out more about the overall arena of horticulture like a detective on a mission, I looked into Fox Valley Tech. I've always been adventurous enough to explore little mysteries in life. At times you could say I've spent too much time exploring and not enough time grounding myself in productivity. Well, this time my adventure turned into a connection worth all the effort in finding it. That connection was packaged as a relationship of a lifetime in a man named, Jim Beard.

Consider a nail-biting Super Bowl that goes down to the final seconds after two teams exchange leads throughout the game. The ups and downs for your team or even just for football fans during a game like this keeps everyone glued to the television. Our society has coined these kinds of events as "instant classics." In other words, they'll be instantaneously remembered and talked about for a long time. In addition to sports, you'll hear this phrase used in association with music and motion pictures once in a while as well.

What's cool is I found an "instant classic" during my very first horticulture class with Jim Beard. One of the first things he said in front of new students was, "Before you can grow plants, I need to grow you as people." Wow, I'm in! What an "instant classic" of a saying. No, this likely won't turn into a popular movie or hit TV show, but I find it rather ironic that the concept is now a book.

I never fathomed an educational experience could be so real and so surreal all at the same time. Jim makes it all real by putting you in positions to apply your skills in initiatives for other organizations. That's real-world experience with no bells and whistles—just practical, hands-on work in which you're knee-deep in everything from planning, designing, constructing, planting, and yes… conversing with people in the community. What a green light to grow as a person! My classrooms for the most part have been out and about in the real world.

Jim is a handshake away from his next relationship. It's that simple. He grows people by mobilizing the value of a handshake and a relationship. Our world is so high-tech that Jim's style of building a community and growing people may seem outdated. Conversely, his style is amazingly effective today. While our society is off texting and inundating itself with another Facebook post, Jim is out putting a face with a name. He's building trust, learning the needs of others, and instituting good. He spends his time sharing a laugh versus typing a smiley face on email.

It's all real with Jim Beard and the opportunities he provides for students are experiential.

Now, the surreal. It's found in the how you go about your business as a student under Jim's mentorship. The connotation of surreal in this breath speaks to the fantastic experiences in which you will find yourself in at times. He gives back to his students through the coattails of his relationships.

You will not receive a silver spoon, however, to go along with your coattail order. Jim's style at times is to lead you to a firehose for a drink. In other words, students will take on experiences that they could only dream of participating in with a high degree of personal accountability and independence. To grow under the Jim Beard model first means you have to grow up. No political correctness with him… and I'm all for that. There is enough of that going on already and where then is leadership?

For example, once Jim and some students were going to provide microgreens for a partner of the college. Jim has established so many partnerships for FVTC that it would make your head spin trying to account for them. The micros didn't grow as anticipated… it happens. That's what learning is all about.

Rather than informing the partner that we regrettably wouldn't be able to offer these provisions, which is professional, Jim said that wasn't good enough. This matter was not about the fact that the partner wouldn't understand or another arrangement couldn't be made—it was all about taking care of the expectation. The partner was looking forward to the greens and for some reason on this rare occasion Jim and the students couldn't deliver due to a glitch in growing.

Dan and Mason are now both enjoying careers in horticulture.

Jim could have had one of his students call and apologize—that's happened before and is a noble, professional gesture as part of both the learning process and the management of relational business best practices. This stuff happens every day to no one's direct fault. Again, all part of the growing process as people is what we're talking about here. Another alternative is that Jim could have called this person directly.

Well, Jim took it one step further than that option. He got in his car and drove to a local organic marketplace and purchased microgreens. He then delivered them to his colleague and partner of the college, disclosing to him that, "We'll take care of you next time." The individual told Jim that he didn't have to go out of his way to do this. Jim replied, "We promised these greens and here are some from XYZ, friend. We'd like you to let us know what ours taste like next time, but for now, enjoy these from a terrific store."

Whatever Jim does with his students evolves around gaining positive exposure for the college and its Horticulture department. In fact, he's on TV a lot! Admirably, he knows the college is not in the position to grow plants for profit like a retail store on a regular basis, although our students do some of this throughout the year as a club fundraiser in Roxanne Rusch-Olesen's class—Jim's fellow Horticulture instructor. In this particular case with the colleague and subsequent trip to an organic marketplace, Jim wanted someone to taste the pride of his students, that's all. At the same time, he's testing the quality of his program's greens and gaining feedback from others. It just didn't turn out as planned, but he made something work for his colleague.

You see, Jim wants the public to know about the "real" and "surreal" stuff that his students are doing to improve lives around the area because he loves his job and the college. Word of mouth travels fast. The best method is to bring people over to see the work at the Service Motor Company Agriculture Center—then they're hooked. If that doesn't happen, Jim can direct people to the numerous structural landmarks around the region in which he has built with FVTC students.

In the aforementioned case with the microgreens and colleague, Jim was also patronizing a local business in which he has tremendous respect for. In fact, in going above and beyond for this partner, Jim opened up another referral for that organic marketplace and this individual. Above and beyond, no excuses, integrity, and ethics… all characteristics that Jim lives by on a daily basis. Imagine what that one extra step did for his relationship with that partner—not to mention a life lesson for the students.

You never know what positive, spontaneous experiences are on the horizon with Jim Beard. In summer of 2014, I was in another surreal moment with him. He was giving a tour of FVTC's greenhouses with a young man and his father. I assumed it was a potential student checking out our labs, grounds, and growing facilities with a parent. You see that kind of thing every day at this college; it is a world class place, really—no matter what program of study.

Jim introduced me to Mr. B. and his father. You could absorb the pride in Jim when he introduced me. That wowed me. He felt so honored to introduce me to Mr. B. and his dad.

When Mr. B. and his father departed that day, Jim said the young man would be starting soon. "Fall semester, Jim?" I naturally asked. "No, his own semester," he replied with a smile. I'm thinking, 'Man, this college does it again. Now that's flexible learning.' Jim elaborated, "Mr. B. is delightful, isn't he? You can tell there's something special about him."

Jim explained that he was coming to FVTC under a special arrangement as a special needs autistic student (not for credit, but for the experience). He wanted me to be part of his team to teach Mr. B. about plants and acclimate him to the school. I was as speechless as I was honored—another surreal, yet authentic moment in education. People are real no matter their circumstance and all learning is real no matter if it is credit based or not.

When Jim mentioned being part of a team, he meant TEAM! He enlisted the help of someone from the college's special needs department to guide us along in working with an autistic individual, formed a team of students—mostly myself and a peer of mine, Dan (from just before me in this chapter), along with Jim and other colleagues. Mr. B. is also accompanied each time he visits the college with a very nice caseworker, who too, is stellar in giving us appropriate guidance.

You know that you're maturing when you start to make sense of frustrations and then turn them into opportunities.

In the early stages of working with Mr. B. at times it was frustrating. It wasn't because of him, but rather due to the stress of getting work done on top of this set up. Dan and I both received one of those "I got it moments" from Mr. B.'s trials and tribulations at the outset of this collaboration. You know that you're maturing when you start to make sense of frustrations and then turn them into opportunities. Had Dan and I not endured a pre-existing relationship and mentorship from Jim prior to working with Mr. B., we'd be telling a different story here.

The "I got it moment" collectively from Dan and me was to have Mr. B. shadow us more than actually work on stuff. Even though we thought he was ready to work, looking back I don't believe the relationship was cemented yet enough for him to trust us in doing work. It's like we were trying to send a wide receiver out for a pass without knowing who his quarterback is. There was no relationship and framework for a team in place yet—lessons well learned!

Mr. B.'s smiles mean he's getting it! Those smiles also draw you in close to him. I feel like his

protector—his big brother. When I walk in the halls, he follows me because there is trust. It humbles me. Those journeys we take around the center and greenhouses protrude confidence in Mr. B. He is no longer nervous or overly excited that much anymore around others.

I'm pursuing more education at FVTC right now, and thankfully that extra time at the college will give me a chance to see Mr. B. once in a while. He's certainly changed my life as did the one who put me in front of him—Jim Beard. When you think about it, Jim's got quite an inventive system in place to grow people. He grows his students, who in turn, grow others. It's a cyclical, self-sustaining people machine of goodness in a tough world. Now that's a difference maker.

One of my treasured memories of working with Jim was when I maintained the organic gardens at FVTC in the summer of 2014. He shared with me one day that a family was hungry and struggling to put food on the table. Without hesitation, we gathered up some vegetables for this family. We helped them get through a tough stretch. No questions, no excuse analyzing—we just did a good deed because it was the right thing to do. We can't solve the world's hunger problems, but we solved a small slice of it so a family could get through a difficult time.

Jim opened my eyes to what success can mean and the different ways in which it can be attained. He cares about those who enter his life beyond explanation. I start my day all the time with this in mind from Jim: *When you work for pay you are feeding your life, but when you work for free or to help others, you are feeding your soul.*

Earlier in this narrative I referenced there was something more to the concept of horticulture than just plants. I believe I have found an answer to that mystery.

4 Gone Nurturing

A mind swimmer is harvesting humanity.

Hard work and setting goals put Catherine "Cat" Mackie in positions to forge life-changing relationships.

Those moments when we make a mess where clutter has no business being are handled differently by everyone. Some have no tolerance for a kitchen table being used as a staging area for a fairy tale rummage sale or an end table in the family room serving as a vertical library. For others, such multi-use furniture and structures are just a "give me a moment to take my breath" rest stop along the way in life to where these culprits of chaos are really heading. It's not that these individuals are necessarily messy or disorganized; it's that they're caught in thought… the Albert Einstein persona of a mind that is always swimming.

For Catherine "Cat" Mackie, countless sheets of paper and piles of pond sketches consumed her parents' beautiful Oriental rugs on a lazy Sunday afternoon. For the Cooksville, Wisconsin native, this was her natural way of spending leisure time.

She found puttering in design and doodling plans for greenspaces entertaining—even though for Cat, her fiddling with these sketches had yet to harvest a sense of direction on where to take this passion as a workplace venture.

For the moment, however, that was OK for Cat. It was her form of getting away to some place she wanted to be. When we have a passion for something, there is no need to question its objective… affinity breeds realization when it's ready to do so. Maybe this gorgeous rug was transforming into inspiration for Cat Mackie.

Cat's Sunday afternoons of leisure were about the only form of downtime for the busy finance professional. If that was her way of relaxing; imagine what she did while working! Jim Beard and I often refer to these types of people as mind swimmers—those who are always swimming with thoughts in their minds. Jim and I are mind swimmers. We often joke that real downtime for us is a nap. That's how you have to shut it off sometimes, really.

The majority of Cat's days in 2007, aside from spending weekends drafting sketches for a "someday" opportunity to design picturesque landscapes and garden getaways, were comprised of working for a payroll and 401K administration company in northeast Wisconsin. She had spent her fair share of years turning pages in overpriced textbooks to earn a Bachelor's degree in Environmental Science, which helped her land the job. She admittedly stayed at the company because of the people, not the work. Knowing that her ultimate livelihood would need to include people was a realization that helped Cat define a new direction. Her passion for people and a drive to further explore landscape design jumpstarted a time for change.

In and out of considering the pursuit of a master's degree, Cat struggled to hang on to a single goal. She's a hardworking, mind swimmer with a strong commitment to doing any job above expectations. Those traits are a dream come true for most hiring managers; yet, at times it poses frustrations for Cat or anyone else who possesses these characteristics. Mind swimmers struggle with direction because they tend to want to do it all.

For starters, Cat wanted to go into business management or study aquaculture. This decision is like selecting a vacation destination in which half the family is looking at Yellowstone Park and the other half is thinking downtown New York City. Leave it up to Cat to make sense out of two opposite concepts, at least "on paper," to reach a feasible career decision.

Cat's new career path ironically didn't include either of those two options—at least for the time being. Now, there's a simple strategy for a mind swimmer: Go with something completely different from an original plan. Such a diverted course also caused Cat to slow down a bit to evaluate life. Remember the messy Oriental rug full of papers? Cat was again doing the same thing… finding value and entertainment in something, but this time it was in the form of structured learning again. No master's degree or double major at a four-year university though— now her "slow start" was taking a community class at Fox Valley Technical College in 2010.

The low-key, exploratory non-credit class offered by Jim Beard during the evening was basically an informal way for anyone to gain general knowledge on how to solve any number of personal gardening issues. The class also enabled Cat to keep working at the finance company during the day. Months later, Cat then took a couple of unrelated touch-and-go classes at FVTC to coincide with her energetic, yet still not-so-orchestrated quest, to find a career path.

Two years later after getting a taste of hands-on education, Cat mustered enough courage to leave her steady job and delve into the green industry by enrolling in FVTC's Horticulture Technician program. She didn't want to job hop as a shot-in-the-dark approach to finding a career passion, but her love for plants and landscaping kept her focused. Ironically, the program's lead instructor was Jim Beard, the same person whom she met in her first class at FVTC two years earlier.

The first thing that struck Cat about Jim when she first met him was his artistic ability. With just a few swift strokes of a Sharpie ® marker on onion-skin paper, Jim showed students how to turn rough sketches into graceful arches and complete designs. For Cat, that evening class paid a lot of dividends. She knew, for starters, that those times when her parents' Oriental rug took on a life of its own as a blueprint table were starting to pay off. She also learned that if she could enhance her designs in a simplistic method due to Jim's instruction, then intuitively Cat would look to FVTC for more direction.

Cat believed it was a calling to do more under the guidance of Jim and others at the college because of those earlier experiences. Chalk one up for the mind swimmer… her pathway to get in the program five years after graduating from a university was not without meaning, purpose, and a few "messy" moments along the way. It didn't happen by throwing a dart against the wall.

In that first program class, Cat recalls Jim's modesty. She addressed him as, "Professor Beard." Jim chuckled and said he didn't have enough years of education to qualify as a professor. What he did have were life experiences and skill, and according to Cat, that was what she needed at this stage in her life. This mind swimmer needed a mentor, not another overpriced textbook.

Cat immediately absorbed the knowledge of the Horticulture Technician program at FVTC. Predictably, her mind raced with fresh ideas on when, where, and how she was going to apply this playground of intelligence. Going into the program, Cat was fairly certain she wanted to customize her learning experiences into a career path of designing water features. Jim lent his ear to her goal with pragmatic reservations. That direct dialogue was an X-factor, or supplemental piece of relevant advice that she wouldn't have received in a textbook—nor was she used to such a style of communication.

"Jim kept me grounded," says Cat. "He never said the water garden niche was bad; he simply shared his experience about the industry as being kind of a vanishing trend (it was now becoming more of an integrated component to comprehensive landscape packages). I had to broaden my scope beyond exclusively looking at water features."

Part of a broadened perspective for a mind swimmer like Cat means opportunity, not just change. She was mature enough to know that change was not always a bad thing, and now she was more mindful to know that Jim was all about opportunity.

Jim's credo of growing people before they grow plants and construct landscape concepts is all about action. Action pays dues. One almost has to witness this approach in order to understand its significance. He doesn't teach or lead as a "one size fits all" figure head. He takes a student or an individual's interests and plucks those aspirations into real-life occasions to put them to work. Granted, a little pain and

A part-time management position in the Visitor Center at Green Bay Botanical Garden and urban forestry work with Ranger Services keep Catherine "Cat" Mackie busy growing people.

some orange barrels figuratively lie ahead in the form of detours and challenges under Jim's model, but by day's end, people grow holistically, not just educationally.

Cat received Jim's pep talk on broadening her outlook with an open mind, and it forced a little patience in her as well—always a hard thing to instill in a mind swimmer. It wasn't until partway through Jim's Landscape Management class at FVTC that Cat sparked an unexpected interest. His class introduced successful landscape owners to the students on a regular basis through either guest speaking or trips to industry establishments; Jim has quite a circle of colleagues. Cat soon realized that an earlier aspiration to own a landscape installation company was now shifting to owning a different type of business: landscape maintenance of botanical or event rental gardens.

> **Granted, a little pain and some orange barrels figuratively lie ahead in the form of detours and challenges under Jim's model, but by day's end, people grow holistically, not just educationally.**

Despite a business plan assignment flopping in an entrepreneur class at FVTC, Cat took the project as a self-analysis of how little she actually knew about the business world. While some students would have thrown their hands up in despair as a result of this event, Cat

pulled up her boot straps and decided to take an entire semester's worth of business classes.

Cat's renewed focus lead her down a number of modified approaches toward taking a second crack at a business plan. Each class added an invaluable piece of the puzzle toward developing a business plan that was not only feasible for industry, but one that she could latch onto with confidence. Notably, Cat understands her business desires are a number of years away from reality. If they fail, she's at peace knowing that her journey in giving it a try will at

Cat loves sharing her passion for plants and landscaping with others.

the very least produce a whole bunch of continued learning experiences, new relationships, some pretty fantastic gardens, and a great location for a retirement home someday. What an attitude for today's world, huh?

"I'm a very different person today than I was when I first stepped into Jim's 'for-the-community' landscaping lecture eight years ago," proclaims Cat. Let's find out who that different person is.

Harvesting Humanity

Cat Mackie's journey brought her a self-proclaimed acceptance of who she is. Hang on… it's hard to not want to stay with the character she portrayed during an eight-year stint in coming into a time of self-discovery. If you're a mind swimmer, you smile along the way at the inundation of thoughts; if you're not a mind swimmer, you maybe picked up an idea or two, or if you're reading for any other purpose, we trust you're engaged for sake of growing people.

Cat began harvesting her green thumb skills to humanity while serving in the student-led Horticulture Club at Fox Valley Technical College, which included one year as its president. During the time she was growing as a person at FVTC, Cat led a couple of original projects for the club under the tutelage of Roxanne Rusch-Olesen. The students hosted a booth at local community events to teach parents of young children about organic composting as a family activity. They also designed a landscaping site with the planting of fresh foliage for the Fox Valley Warming Shelter, a nonprofit agency that provides basic needs services to help people achieve levels of self-sufficiency. All said and done, Cat had more than doubled the attendance of the Horticulture Club as well from previous years.

Jim's philosophy of learning gives you a general sense of an objective that takes you on a stumble-and-correct mission as compared to following steps. While frustrating at times, it forces people to think for themselves as they work toward an end goal. The frustration actually functions as a gut check in how to use soft skills and adaptation proficiencies to find the root of one's anxiety. Was it something technical, mathematical, etc., or did a student shortcut a process or simply not listen or ask a question versus assuming something? Life skills.

> What Jim's essentially doing is a little nurturing on the front end of a lesson with an expectation that students need to establish their own way of thinking. He has you slow down to set sub goals along the way to reaching bigger ones. It's tough, but very empowering at the end.

See where passing life skills along to others by way of learning under Jim's model is a slam dunk for community prosperity? For example, Cat recalls working in a garden during her studies with Jim. He provided species photos and some basic guidelines in working with plants. From there, students needed to get their hands dirty. To reach an end result (harvest for fruits and vegetables or healthy beautification for flowers, plants, shrubs, and trees, etc.), students were expected to exercise hands-on knowledge in initial planning stages from planting to nurturing initial growth to maintaining mature plants and features… a process.

If the outcomes related to harvest or beautification were compromised along the way, it's a student's responsibility to go back and fix them, according to Cat. There won't be much hand holding; there will be plenty of reminders about quality and communication. "Think about that," she says. "What Jim's essentially doing is a little nurturing on the front end of a lesson with an expectation that students need to establish their own way of thinking. He has you slow down to set sub goals along the way to reaching bigger ones. It's tough, but very empowering at the end."

Through it all, Cat has landed on her feet from immersing herself in several life-changing projects in the program and by taking business classes at FVTC. She developed a management style that leads from within—first by passing the baton of club presidency in the form of "co-presidency" so a new leader would not be immediately overwhelmed with the new role.

This fresh way of transitioning the reigns of leadership let Cat (and future club presidents who turn over the responsibility) take a step back to watch a new club president ride the coattails of what was already done into other endeavors or as a continuation of existing accomplishments. It was the implementation of a mentor-based passing of the baton that supplied a new leader with a foundation. Cat basically helped harvest the next generation of leaders for the club through this new systematic improvement.

At this time Cat was working part-time for a landscaping firm while studying two different academic pathways and leading the Horticulture Club... all in a day's work for a mind swimmer, right? When Cat left her job for a new, full-time position in September 2014 for college supporter and adjunct instructor Dan Traas at Ranger Services, a nearby urban forestry and landscape management consulting firm, she harvested humanity again to make sure her former employer had a crop of skilled talent to fill the void she left. How many times do you see that happen these days?

With an exciting new career in hand that is much closer to where her mind was more than eight years ago on an Oriental rug full of landscape sketches, Cat has arrived to greener pastures. She attributes a lot of her new direction and success to Jim and

his opening of doors to industry colleagues. In fact, that same landscape management class mentioned earlier opened up an additional opportunity for Cat as a weekend manager at Green Bay Botanical Gardens to accompany her new full-time career.

That opportunity surfaced while Cat was researching the intricacies of green growing spaces as they relate to botanical garden concepts as part of a class project. Cat came across a job posting for the position on a whim while checking out the nonprofit organization's web site. Although she didn't need the job, Cat was called to it because of Jim's strong relationship with the organization—it was like, "I think I better take this as a chance to learn how management plays a role in this field."

Smart is as smart does. The weekend management position is a great way for Cat to involve herself in an experience that will directly contribute to her entrepreneurial goal of owning an event rental garden business someday. The whole process of attending FVTC and working with Jim and his co-faculty member, Roxanne, was like a well-oiled machine that orchestrates plans of success for students. Orchestrates? Funny... mind swimmers often jump in without much navigation. Remember Cat's days without much orchestration?

Now that Cat is on a defined, structured path toward success... who knows how much humanity will benefit from her skill along the way. The bottom line is society is better off when after growing people... it passes the baton on to grow others in the footsteps of good.

5 Outdoor Giving

A project man beautifies exteriors for others.

Retirement means learning more and giving extra for Bill Henry.

Bill Henry has never been one to let any grass grow under his feet. Nearing retirement, this engineering veteran of the paper and converting industry has seen his fair share of endless sales calls, configuring Computer-Aided Design (CAD) schemes for no two companies alike, and growing relationships. Today, the president of Advance Systems, Inc. in De Pere, Wisconsin is finally allowing for a little grass to grow "around" his feet while he takes a love for detail outside the walls of corporate America.

For Bill, puttering around the house over the years as a self-proclaimed "project man" conjured up a few stumbling moments while he immersed himself as a makeshift plumber, electrician, or craftsman. His wife, Fran, has often jokingly reminded him not to confuse confidence with competence. At the same time, Fran has admired Bill's perseverance toward taking on projects that he's never attempted before. Bill would often say that his lack of experience in many "handyman" areas was good for the economy

because he made an insane number of trip to places like Home Depot, venturing down aisles he has never been before.

This whimsical and enduring dynamic where Fran serves as a domestic advisor to her project man recently sprung an idea for the empty nesters of the same house for 35 years. Fran and Bill found a new lot to build a home better suited for their needs at this point in life. For the project man, it was time to learn the ropes of doing stuff outside as opposed to inside since the lot needed some work. Here comes another task that was never attempted before by Bill—look out green light specials at local hardware stores!

Another never-attempted-before task was now on Bill's radar concerning a new home and underdeveloped lot. The lessons learned over the years as a project man rang in a little reality for Bill thanks to Fran's insight from her years working at Fox Valley Technical College (FVTC). Anyone heading off into the sunset after working at FVTC would have to be blindfolded every day during his or her career not to notice the exterior beauty from those who toil in green around the Appleton campus.

Students, summer landscaping crews, and others connected to the Horticulture program at FVTC dish out instant memories for anyone visiting or working there, day in and day out (seasonally speaking, of course, we're talking about Wisconsin). You just can't ignore the green goodness at this campus. Its structures, like the Hartling Family Rose Garden, have been highlighted nationally in *USA Today*, and the menagerie of plants and trees pull people in for a deeper look. It's not unusual to see students reading a book under a shade tree or near a designed waterfall structure—let alone visitors bent over to gain a closer glimpse of gorgeous greens.

Armed with her own memories of FVTC's exterior wonder and looking ahead to their new lot, Fran suggested to Bill that he take a landscape design course with Jim Beard at the college. Personally from working in higher education for more than a decade, it's somewhat rare to hear someone say, "Take a course with so and so" as opposed to just, "Take an XYZ course."

Jim's reputation supersedes any class name. He's earned that level of precedence. His style of relationship building is a dying breed, but ironically it's powerfully effective today more than ever while most everyone else is tweeting, talking about when they're going to mow their grass on Facebook, and doing selfies. He's all about substance in an era of what feels good. Jim places people before technology, and his style still has a place in the sun—perhaps more significantly than we would admit by today's standards.

Bill jumped into the six-week course and quickly realized he was in the right place. He recalls an instant admiration for Jim, which reaffirmed the reason why his wife and many others associate learning with a person (in this case, Jim)—not a course name or number. "It was evident Jim knew his business, but I was drawn to him because of his unassuming and quizzical nature," says Bill. "He wasn't there to tell me what I wanted to know or what made him look good. He was there to provide the basic tenants of design, offer insight, and let the rest play out."

To Bill's surprise, he learned that effective landscaping included a number of key fundamentals that extend beyond design proficiency. That's quite a startling development when you consider 44 years of success in engineering. Concepts like beauty, texture, compatibility, function, durability, and strength, to name a few, all go into the heart of world class landscape structures. These competencies got Bill even more excited about how he was going to apply his new skills on those never-done-before tasks.

"I discovered a whole new level of confidence from watching Jim pull together all these elements into a process of making one heck of a structure," notes Bill. "It's apparent he is an artist trapped in an engineer's mind, and that's a winning combination for landscape design."

> It's apparent he [Jim] is an artist trapped in an engineer's mind, and that's a winning combination for landscape design.

Then life gets busy—such is the case for most working professionals these days. Those at-home projects get tabled while making ends meet takes priority. Fran and Bill had their plan in place for a new home; however, it sat on the back burner for seven years. When Fran and Bill finally realized it was time to put that goal into action in 2014, the couple revisited where they left off. Enter the outdoor lot project once again.

Enamored with excitement to learn something from Jim Beard once again, Bill sought his notes from the earlier landscape design class seven years ago. The problem was those notes were nowhere to be found. 'No problem,' thought Bill, 'It will be both fun and a useful refresher to take the course again.' He signed up for Jim's class, but not the *same class*. Bill mistakenly registered for Landscape Construction at FVTC instead of Landscape Design—the previous class in which he gained a lot of knowledge from.

Bill didn't realize his error until he was in class the first night and heard Jim discuss the course objectives focusing on "hardscapes" such as arbors, retaining walls, patio pavers, and such. Laughing inside at himself, Bill stayed for the whole session and quickly discovered a bunch of fresh outdoor project ideas for the new lot.

Like the design class, Jim still encouraged creativity in the study of landscape construction… that helped Bill reflect on some prior learning experiences at FVTC. Jim also underscored a dose of discipline to accompany anyone's use of creativity in this field. Bill mentioned that Jim did a solid job of painting a picture that landscape construction resembled "outdoor furniture" with city codes, proper drainage systems, ergonomic functionality, durability, and

more all playing as factors in practicality. This is a far cry from putting in some cool-looking berms in a backyard.

Bill found himself surrounded by several students in their twenties who were attending class for a different reason. These students aspired to making a career out of their horticulture studies at FVTC. Jim made a point to the class that for every **how to** there is a **why for**. In other words, how to make something has a direct impact on **why** it's being done and **for** whom. This moment struck Bill. He knew there was a reason for that error in class registration. Bill did end up taking Landscape Design anyway right after this class (as a side note)!

Take It Outside

According to Bill, Jim Beard's **how to** and **why for** instructional technique is so simple that it's brilliant. It prepares students for what employers are looking for in the industry and further develops them into thinking like professionals. Come to think of it, as Bill emphasizes, this approach is universally viable in any instructional setting. Bill said Jim used the example of doing precision stone work as a path. The finished product should be level with tight, accentuated borders.

A finished project of this magnitude should also be so clean that someone who looks at a stone pathway should immediately want to walk on it. The **how to** in this case is not so much about "how to do something" as it is "how to distinguish yourself"

Bill Henry built a getaway space at Iris Place for those who could use a little relaxation in their day.

from other job prospects while applying new skills. For the end user of our stone path example, the walkway is unlike no other in the eyes of those who frequent it for whatever reason. The cherry atop this technique to Jim's teaching of landscape design and construction is evident in how he also grows careers for people and builds structures for industry; they are both exceptional. Any student in his class is going to be one well-rounded individual when he or she finishes college, and any organization blessed enough to receive his work is going to be showing off something exemplary. Quality in America is found right in Appleton, Wisconsin in Jim Beard's indoor and outdoor classrooms.

Moved by these kinds of "unadvertised benefits" in taking Jim Beard's courses, Bill set his sights beyond tackling never-done-before projects by taking his talents outside with an unwavering desire to put them to use anywhere. Inspired to do more after taking care of home base in that new lot by building a pergola, two raised garden beds, and a decorative stone wall, Bill started his own tour of growing people. The project man is now full of confidence in tasks of the unknown. Plans are underway to add a terraced rose garden, walkway, and water feature on the new lot. A little Fran and a pinch of Jim Beard have concocted the ingredients for a landscape machine in the form of Bill Henry!

Be careful what you ask for. In the past year, several of his new neighbors have noticed Bill's craftsmanship. He suspects a little consulting is on the horizon, but for now, he can prolong the neighbors a bit by

slowly bringing them into the mix of his new passion— Bill caught the bug for landscape construction and he's hit the road to change a few lives in need of basic services first.

Bill's engineering background combined with rubbing elbows with Jim Beard has set the stage for more people growing in the community. He recognizes a need that many non-profit organizations have for upgrades in landscaping or even hardscaping. Budget constraints typically move these needs to the bottom of the priority list for nonprofits, rightfully so, since most of them typically put their money to work for direct human services.

That said, the outdoor ambiance of some non-profit organizations has a direct influence on the psychological and physical wellbeing of their clientele. For example, shelters, respite centers, and transitional housing units rely on exterior beautification and upkeep as a central piece of therapy and restoration

The new pergola at Iris Place in Appleton

concerning the health and outlook of those they serve. Again, non-profit funds are tight and volunteers, bless their hearts, are limited in skill sets when it comes to landscape design and construction.

Jim's classes gave Bill a taste of this type of real-world, real-time philanthropy. Bill was part of a team of students who worked on a courtyard for Lincoln Elementary School in Appleton and an outdoor makeover at Brewster Village—highlighted earlier in this book. Now, out and about with his own green landscaping thumb while easing into retirement, Bill reconstructed a pergola at Iris Place, a peer-run respite for individuals experiencing emotional distress or crisis. The safe haven is a program of NAMI Fox Valley—a local affiliate of the National Alliance on Mental Illness.

Iris Place offers around-the-clock support by a trained and caring staff, all of whom have lived experience with mental illness and/or substance abuse. That support now comes with a view of tranquility thanks to Bill's time and talent. The pergola stands tall and peacefully in the backyard of the historic building where Iris Place resides. Growing people sometimes means growing their spirits first, and the pergola functions as a reflective getaway.

Right out of Jim Beard's playbook on growing people, Bill has enlisted the help of other volunteers to join in and have fun, learn, contribute, and "grow." When the Iris Place project is finished, Bill will take his outdoor endeavors to put in a pergola and a pathway at the Outagamie County Cemetery in Grand Chute. That site is a final resting place for 135 residents of the former Outagamie County Asylum for the Chronically Insane, which was founded in 1889 just to the south of FVTC's Appleton campus.

Over its 112-year history, the asylum underwent many changes. It closed in 1943 and the building was finally demolished in 2001 and replaced by the bright and modern facility known today as Brewster Village (what a tie in to this book). The asylum's cemetery is located on what is now the south side of FVTC's Appleton campus, where it borders a vehicle training range for truck driving students.

The cemetery was not used after 1943 and since that time has been largely neglected and forgotten. Yet for the past 10 years, Jim Beard and his students each year have taken on the duty under their own volition of mowing the grass and caring for the property out of respect for its resting souls. Recently, the State and County approved a plan on behalf of a group of concerned citizens to permanently restore the cemetery. That initiative will include a memorial, pergola, and other landscaping features to help give it a permanent, proper designation.

Bill looks forward to being part of that project as well in the very near future. After all, the project man has grown himself. His volunteer work is not only growing people, he is growing souls. He also looks forward to those surprise visits by Jim Beard, who will joyfully infuse Bill with a few personal tips and point out the virtues of the 3-4-5 triangle.

Until Jim visits again, Bill propels forward with lasting impressions from him as a remembrance to what learning under Jim's tutelage has meant, personally and for the community. Bill now draws greater meaning to a few memorable moments with Jim and his students.

"I often wanted to take the lead on projects during class because of my age and experience," says Bill. "One day a team member of mine, a fellow student, was just about to cut a final piece of wood for a project… but from the wrong end. Jim was looking right at him, and I was surprised that he did not correct the young man. He let the student make the mistake."

Bill shared that the student learned the lesson of "measure twice, cut once" as impressed upon by Jim Beard as a method of teaching construction. Catchy sayings mean nothing on their own—you have to put them to work and experience a result, according to Jim and witnessed first-hand by Bill. "Growing people" is more important than keeping a self-imposed schedule, and that lesson is contagious to Bill as he works with more and more individuals who turn their green thumbs into something wonderful for all to enjoy.

Bill feels a sense of urgency in his community based on time spent with Jim Beard. "We all can't live forever, and if people need a little direction in life, by God, hang out with Jim Beard for a while, and somehow, some way, he will make you a better person," affirms Bill.

> **We all can't live forever, and if people need a little direction in life, by God, hang out with Jim Beard for a while, and somehow, some way, he will make you a better person.**

"One time a student learned from a guest speaker in class how he became a supervisor in the industry in less than four years. The guest said he probably only worked 2% more than the others before becoming a supervisor. He continued to disclose that while others took breaks, he simply walked around to get to know people with a positive attitude. That little bit of extra work, relationship building, and upbeat attitude landed him a job as a supervisor. Jim Beard creates those types of moment for his students; it's up to them to do to the rest."

(in Bill's voice)... Two percent, huh? That was an X-factor in life for the guest speaker in Jim's class. Chris Jossart teaches X-factor mobilization; Jim puts you in positions to find them—what a team, these two. *(end of Bill's voice)*

The project man's personal transition into a "people grower" contains the imparting of both project skills and life skills. Bill Henry tips his hat to Jim Beard for awakening an appreciation of humor, patience, and empathy within a learning process. To Bill, the original 'people grower' was born a teacher... Jim ensures that each student carries a torch of soft skills along with his or her technical aptitude.

Bill Henry's story introduces yet another snapshot of what personal growth can look like within our pool of already outstanding green baton passers featured thus far in *Growing People: How green landscapes and garden spaces can change lives*. A bit more experienced than traditional students and closing in on retirement, Bill epitomizes how horticulture and landscaping is a prime outlet for anyone looking at "what to do next in life" once retired. His confidence, life experiences, goal-setting, and maturation are foregone conclusions as to the value he brings to his community.

Bill is a poster child regarding how one's time in retirement years can make a huge dent in the lives of others through tinkering in green. If Jim Beard had 100 "Bill Henrys" at his fingertips, our society would be much better off, and you can take that notion to the bank.

One of these days we're going to wake up and find the Fox Valley region is a parade of green people growers and givers like this nation has never seen before... we all can't wait because it can't happen fast enough.

6 Members of Momentous Moments

Green joy is found in every day moments.

Cyndee Smith uses green upgrades to infuse joy for members of the Community Day Center.

Up to this point in *Growing People: How green landscapes and garden spaces can change lives,* we have witnessed simple train-the-trainer accounts on how experiences in horticulture are generating opportunities for personal growth. The process of learning a green-related skill and then sharing that knowledge with others unravels numerous benefits for people and places. Teaching, working, and volunteering in skilled landscaping and gardening drive a perpetual cycle of community development. We are seeing something special going on wherever Jim Beard and his students pop up around town.

Cyndee Smith culminates our stories of growing people a bit differently from those who have preceded her in the book. Prior accounts of individuals touched by Jim Beard and then observing how they've passed the green baton to enrich others' lives have included profiles of horticulturists and skilled landscapers. Cyndee loves flowers and playing in soil more on the hobby side as compared to the rest of our literary content contributors. Her true impact on growing people is by connecting dots that translate into resources to change lives.

It didn't take long to realize that Cyndee's interpersonal style of communication complements her important role as program assistant for the Community Day Center in Appleton, Wisconsin (She doesn't email—how refreshing! If you want to do some business with her, it's face-to-face.). The organization is an affiliate of Valley Packaging Industries, a reputable community provider in guiding people with disabilities to lead more independent lives. The Center provides personalized planning, care, and programming for adult members during the day as respite for their primary caregivers—mostly family members.

(author's note): The Community Day Center is right across the street from... you guessed it, Brewster Village! The Center, Brewster Village, Outagamie County Asylum for the Chronically Insane Cemetery, and Fox Valley Technical College (FVTC) are within walking distance of one another

and all a part of this book! We didn't plan it this way, and if you're ever around the Fox Valley region, pay a visit and bring some people to grow! Perhaps we'll establish some sort of tour marker of sorts where after a half-mile trek visitors will see where a whole bunch of people growing has occurred and continues to happen. *(end of author's note)*

Cyndee had commented on seeing FVTC's Horticulture students next door at Brewster Village. She knew Jim Beard from years ago while seeing his work around the community. The Brewster project subtly reminded her of Jim's community work here and there as she planned to contact him for some light consultation at the Center. It was in need of some green renovations, and Cyndee was welcoming ideas on how to adorn the surroundings of a new pavilion that was put in for members and their families, in addition to her colleagues.

The majority of the Community Day Center's members are challenged by some sort of disability characteristic. They range in age from 18 into their 80s, and some are elderly and frail, while others have moderate-to-profound cognitive impairments. The staff works proactively to make its member programming as experiential as possible. By doing so, members develop or enhance skills in social integration, communication, wellness, and both motor and eye/hand coordination.

The Center's new pavilion was built with a cement foundation in spring of 2013 near the corner of its lot, partially nestled by aged trees and a well-kept lawn. A clear structure of tranquility, the pavilion has been used rather lightly in its first two years with sightings of mostly staff members enjoying break time. It appeared something was missing with the outdoor pavilion. Could it be an absence of allure for members—in whatever way, shape, or form that happened to look like?

Cyndee met with her co-workers at the Center to discuss ways to more adequately use the pavilion for its members. They agreed the structure was being underutilized. Enter Jim Beard. Cyndee contacted Jim and his first visit was in summer of 2013.

The two met at the Community Day Center… a connector of resources got together with a green people grower. Pull up a chair and grab a cup of coffee for this one! On paper, this interaction was a blueprint for anything and everything good to come out of it. Maybe "good" was a lower standard for these two given what was about to transpire. What surfaced from Cyndee and Jim's meeting was a soft crusade to get members engaged in green activities. The pavilion was basically an icebreaker to greater days ahead for the members and overall culture of the Center.

Jim's first visit also included time to get to know the members. They took to him immediately— mostly because of his gentle, expressionistic persona. He provided a brief overview on how plants and garden beds can add further joy to the programs at the Center. Cyndee noted that Jim really had an innate ability to connect with the members. Wisdom is knowing how to take someone who has "been around the block" in life and letting him or her assemble your community.

Wisdom is knowing how to take someone who has "been around the block" in life and letting him or her assemble your community.

The immediate green task for the Community Day Center on behalf of Jim Beard and a few students was the construction of two raised garden beds alongside the pavilion. The beds are anchored by strong, clear borders, and they're easily accessible for members near a door on the side of the building. Jim and Cyndee decided to build the beds close to the main building so members can easily get back and forth with produce, gardening tools, etc. The beds visibly portray that they're part of the pavilion—adding even more "atmosphere" to the structure.

Tomatoes, kale, and peppers originally filled the garden beds that first year in 2013. Members were beginning to latch onto an activity that seemingly could turn into an annual program. Planting, maintenance (weeding, watering, etc.), harvesting, along with seasonal cleanup and preparation conjured up a comprehensive, ongoing activity for years to come.

As the inaugural raised bed growing season neared fruition at the Community Day Center (then known as Valley Packaging Day Services until the name was changed to Community Day Center in 2015), Jim Beard was just getting started all over again with Cyndee Smith as the two began whipping up more green joy for the members. With winter around the corner, both of them thought that seed stratification would serve as a fun offseason and indoor activity for the members.

The late fall project at the Center became known as the sleeping seed project. Jim visited again to meet with the members. He described and demonstrated how different plants can grow effectively as a result of a seasonal sleep-to-grow process. From their earlier interactions with Jim via raised garden beds, the members began to trust him. They looked forward to his visits and formed a level of respect for him. Momentous moments have arrived at the Community Day Center.

Jim's work with the members included a lot of reaffirmation that they had plenty to look forward to in spring from the sleeping seed project. The mature seedlings could then be replanted to wherever the members desired. That seemed to get them thinking enthusiastically about possibilities.

Raised garden beds are the talk of the Community Day Center when it comes to salad time.

At the moment, the members had their own small beds to put the sleeping seeds into. Cyndee observed that those little seeds were nurtured and cared for with a gentle touch—mirroring in some ways how the members are taken care of daily. What an observation. What a testament to the growing culture at the Community Day Center.

After a couple of months, Jim returned and led the next phase of the sleeping seed project. He helped members transfer the now young seedlings into small containers to further spark the growing process for spring. As time progressed, many of the more than a dozen members ultimately worked independently with their seeds and plants as spring of 2014 approached. This was a brand new experience for most of these individuals. Before spring of 2014, Jim would frequent the Center with his green thumb in back pocket. Wait… Jim Beard with green thumb in back pocket? What was going on?

Jim noted that Cyndee did such a fabulous job of guiding the members through the project during the latter winter months that his visits until spring were essentially relational. What was happening is that the growing of people was occurring in optimum capacity. The green people grower was making a difference by just visiting and not really getting hands-on with others around plants and structures like he's been accustomed to. Cyndee, the green baton grower, kept the project moving ahead by providing natural mentorship in the form of basic plant care.

The dynamic between Cyndee and Jim stemmed into a model community program for the Center's members. They started to move a needle in their minds from day-to-day fulfillment toward looking forward to something regular and ongoing from a programming standpoint. It was evident something was gelling. Cyndee realizes that all of the Center's programs and community volunteers add value to its members' experiences, and now she was witnessing Jim basically adopting the place as part of his regular tour of growing people.

The results are nothing short in the meaning of

Cyndee Smith is having the time of her life introducing green concepts to members of the Community Day Center.

life—no matter the circumstance or time. There is no agenda, predetermined plan, or expectation for anything in return. Growing people comes down to making the most of our travels. It doesn't cost anything, is not subjective to political mumbo jumbo (OK, 99% of the time), and the relationships are forever empowering. Think about it… with a nation engulfed in sensationalized headlines and unprecedented generational narcissism, our life's purpose is something we can remain true to.

For the members of the Community Day Center, they took on a sense of ownership over the sleeping seed project. For them, they were growing people (just not directly). Their way of giving back when the plants were big enough was to offer beauty for a "home away from home" or through presenting them to family members or friends.

What a sight it was to see the following spring after the members took care of these seeds over winter! They grew irises, lilies, black-eyed Susans, and a variety of small trees and shrubs for a makeover that enhanced the walk for visitors from the parking lot to the main entrance. The introduction of a new landscape extended along the side of the building's exterior and down a ways near the pavilion.

By the way, ever wonder where Jim gets all these plants? They are mostly given to him by his entourage of industry colleagues all around northeast Wisconsin once he shares how they're going to be used. Greenhouse owners, for instance, who have to make a living basically seven-eight months out of the year, aren't giving here for tax break purposes. They do it knowing that Jim is going to make someone's life better along the way as compared to putting plants up on a silent auction block. Charity is good; growing people is charity.

The Community Day Center's accounts of people growing are even somewhat behind the scenes in terms of its new family of plants. It's like each plant has a story and a destination. In addition, members made several discoveries and attained new skills as a result of beautifying the building's exterior. They learned how to work while wearing gloves and how to use gardening tools. Over time, they watched their efforts turn into splendor. For them, the venture represented a collaborative learning opportunity where they could get some fresh air, use their hands to bring another type of life to the Center, and understand how to care for it.

Everything from working with one's hands to feeling tranquility and seeing colors and beauty, or just being outside around a garden, can all prompt positive memories.

Many of these individuals would literally take a few steps backward in the grass after planting a flower to immediately see success in their work. Some planted flowers in pots, and those members realized that their labor could move around the facility from time to time as well. Those observations would serve as extra reminders about the mark these members were making on their own "home away from home."

For some members, gardening brought back memories of something they once did as a hobby. Members suffering from dementia or another type of memory loss can draw on specific recollections or senses from gardening. Green experiences can lead to remembering certain events in life. Everything from working with one's hands to feeling tranquility and seeing colors and beauty, or just being outside around a garden, can all prompt positive memories.

One day in the summer of 2014 after the first round of foliage was planted near the main entrance, Jim was paying a visit to check out the raised garden beds. While walking toward them from the parking lot, he caught a glimpse of a member standing outside the main entrance doors. It was evident the gentleman was staring at Jim by the way he followed his movements across the lawn. Jim recognized the man from previous visits.

Jim energetically shouted, "Hello" while walking closer toward the pavilion. Moments later, he stopped in his tracks. The gentleman started rubbing his face quite profusely in a motion symbolic to desiring a shave. At first, Jim didn't think anything of it and just stood there smiling at the man in case he wanted to strike up a conversation. He waved and smiled at the man and proceeded toward the pavilion.

Jim returned the next day to deliver some plants. While leaving, he noticed the same man making the identical form of nonverbal communication while waving as a greeting with his other hand. Jim went up and exchanged pleasantries with the member. After one of the Center's employees retrieved the member for a group activity, out of curiosity Jim causally asked her about the man's habitual body language when he's around.

The staff member told Jim that is how the man associates his presence around the Center. Jim's last name began to resonate with this particular newer member from the first day he was introduced to him midway through the sleeping seed project. When he sees Jim, he rubs his face like he is moving his hands over a "beard" (despite not having one). Remember the famous dance song from the mid-90s called the "Macarena" by the band, Los Del Rio? Watch out for a song titled "The Beard" coming to a record store near you.

Another member of the Center likes to hang out by the main entrance in anticipation of Jim's arrival. It took a while for staff members to figure out what was happening. She wanted to learn about gardening so badly that she thought Jim would be visiting on days when he wasn't even expected to be there for perhaps a week or two. Lesson learned: Please use specific days for certain members like "Monday" or "Thursday" when referencing Jim and/or his crew returning.

Kitchen Crusaders

A year after the raised garden beds were constructed at the Community Day Center, Cyndee convened with her team to brainstorm how the new growing contraptions could enhance the members' Kitchen Club. This informal "get involved anytime you want to" each Friday group of members enjoyed making entrees, while learning the importance of washing and cleaning food. The garden beds introduced a seasonal supply of vegetables that were readily accessible. Members could regularly sample tomatoes, kale, and other vegetables and then determine how to integrate them into their dishes.

Kitchen Club members really glommed onto the raised beds. Already versed with a nice dose of culinary aptitude from visiting farmer's markets, making cookies for cookie exchanges, and getting ideas from cooking magazines, these kitchen crusaders quickly made the beds a part of their routine like an avid swimmer would to a pool in the backyard.

Each Friday morning, an announcement is made inviting members to be voluntarily involved in Kitchen Club activities for that day, which often includes making a light lunch or snacks for other members. Salads have become increasingly popular because of the fresh vegetables from the beds. Healthy eating discussions have also frequently made their way into Kitchen Club activities.

"The green additions to the Community Day Center have helped build a distinct community within our family of members, staff, and volunteers," notes Jill Paalman, family liaison manager and Cyndee's immediate supervisor. "A program like this is truly indicative of how someone like Cyndee demonstrates genuine compassion toward the members. It's like they know she is thinking of their best interests."

With approximately one third of the Center's population wheelchair bound, Cyndee believes the organization is on the verge of even more extraordinary offerings for its members. "Jim's garden beds, for example, are something that we're looking forward to further developing as a means to impact more members," she says. "The higher the beds, the less our members have to bend over to garden. Jim has all kinds of tricks of the trade up his sleeve for our members, and we can't wait to see what's in store next for them."

As we speak, Jim is concocting a new design similar to ornamental raised beds for the members of the Community Day Center in his shop tucked away beyond the horizon. The brilliancy of what goes on in that wood shop makes anyone want to be a fly on the wall for just a moment to see this humble person do his thing. While that moment lingers in time, momentous moments dance gleefully at the Center.

Jim's humility spreads like wild fire to those who know (and will know) him. "He is an extension of my job," states Cyndee. "He has assisted us in building a strong culture of learning and giving at the Center, and those attributes extend into the hearts of our members' families and into the community."

Here's food for thought: The members of Valley Packaging's Community Day Center represent the next chapter of green baton passers in growing people. Look at what they've done in growing one another and in raising the quality of life in their community under Cyndee and Jim's partnership. Congratulations, members!

There is no class offered on how to grow people.

There's only class found within those who do it.

UNIT

3

Beds, Bales Buckets, & Brews

Garden with ease by using natural growing systems customized for you and your surroundings courtesy of the Director of Detail.

First, a little business…
DISCLAIMER:

The following steps and general "do-it-yourself" overview of landscape structures and growing systems are presented in Unit 4 of *Growing People: How green landscapes and garden spaces can change lives* under the premise that anyone who uses this subject matter has adequate hands-on knowledge of woodshop equipment, materials, and tools, as well as gardening and material configurations and related measurements.

Moreover, the measurements and configurations associated with the following growing systems and their parts/components are presented as a general guide for others desiring to build them. They are NOT presented as concrete content in the form of instructional steps.

The authors of this literacy work are not responsible for any misuses of said equipment, materials, or tools that relate to the construction or maintenance of any of the following growing systems and their subsidiary parts/components, nor are they responsible for any injuries or death as a result of this content.

The authors highly recommend that anyone desiring to construct one or any of the following growing systems and their subsidiary parts/components consult a more experienced or professional landscape construction worker if his or her knowledge of said subject matter is questionable or absent.

Please exercise caution when using dangerous equipment and tools.

Be smart and be safe.

Thanks.

Jim & Chris

7 Beds of Bloom

Raised garden beds accent outdoor living spaces and bring the gardening experience closer to you.

*Sustainable growing that is easy on the eyes, joints, and back meets exterior design in this first of four chapters set to make you look like a green-thumb champion. The simple steps in this final unit of **Growing People: How green landscapes and garden spaces can change lives** will empower you with do-it-yourself skills. These newfound talents will transcend into simplicity in the garden and reflect a lifestyle that is true to you.*

Any of these projects are ripe for adding personal variations if done so safely. The first of four recent refinements in organic growing systems that Jim, the Director of Detail in this context, has either masterfully crafted or modified with his own personal touch from industry benchmarks is organic raised beds.

Organic raised beds serve as sustainable little gardens that conveniently give gardeners easy access to well-defined, growing spaces. They can essentially go anywhere there is a lawn or natural compost surface, leaving room for lots of creativity in one's yard. These crafted beds also complement commercial spaces. Businesses are catching on to their diverse usefulness. While writing this book, the Director of Detail and his students put in raised garden beds in a courtyard at Appleton Medical Center. The space partially lies between the hospital's cafeteria and main lobby.

These beds can be constructed in a few different sizes. Design latitude gives gardeners several options pertaining to location. An ornamental style raised bed (typically 2 by 2 ft. or larger and is a boxed variation with a bottom and higher walls compared to the model bed that is described in this chapter) is becoming commonplace on back decks, front porches, alongside cement or paved patios, next to tennis courts and swing sets, near mulched trails, and so on. Due to simple assembly, in no time you can build any variation of a raised garden bed to go with those moments when we all think, 'That empty space needs something.'

Some people position raised beds in rows for an organized inventory of green outcomes, and others embed them within their already existing garden

A traditional raised garden bed [25]

or backyard arrangements. The beds also lend themselves to a little aesthetic creativity, if desired. You'll see everything from hand-painted flowers to personalized stickers to colored symbols on the sides of these gardens—even variations of sports team logos have popped up on the sides of raised beds. The beds are not intended to be marketed as free-standing canvases of artistic inspiration; nonetheless, it's nice to see them offer room for some expressionistic freedom once in a while!

In a more natural context, Jim says some gardeners surround the inside perimeter of their raised beds with marigolds for a touch of beauty. Planting petunias near the edges will reveal a covered look as they'll climb over the sides to add an element of drapery against the walls of the beds. He's even seen some with other structures erected on the inside, like hanging baskets and garden flags. The

possibilities for a reflection of you are endless with raised garden beds.

While Jim's following of plant lovers continues to grow each year during his lectures about as fast as fans wearing Aaron Rodgers jerseys around here, awareness of raised beds is growing, too. Incidentally, these beds vary mostly in height—so their appearance presents a diverse look at plant stations, greenhouses, and so forth. Ornamental raised beds, for instance, can range from two-to-three feet-plus in height and are almost completely closed at the bottom (again, unlike the ones described by Jim in just a bit—those are shorter and open at the bottom to connect with nature's nutrients). Any type of a raised bed is built with either rough sawn cedar or rough Douglas fir cedar.

Jim introduced the ornamental raised beds to the community in 2011 as part of an internal partnership with Fox Valley Technical College's Occupational Therapy Assistant (OTA) program. The collaboration once again combined the skills of horticulture students with people from another entity to better someone, somewhere. These beds are a bit more mobile (when empty) and stand higher for people suffering from severe orthopedic-related issues. The OTA students used the beds as part of a semester-long study on leisure, movement, and pain management. A limited number of ornamental beds were made in the spring of 2011, and they were sold to the public as a student club fundraiser.

And did they sell! More than half were gone from word of mouth before a public sale occurred on a Saturday morning. When that event started, the ornamental raised beds all sold out in the first half hour. Ornamental beds haven't been made as part of a class project since that time due to broader community-wide projects within the Horticulture Technician program at FVTC, but this partnership

> **When that event started, the ornamental raised beds all sold out in the first half hour.**

was a huge success in many ways. Jim just smiled when the effort concluded and said, "Growing people without even trying."

An ornamental style raised garden bed

Regardless of the type of raised bed, they have added benefits beyond joint and back preservation. Their confined and well-defined space contains all the elements of optimal growing right under a gardener's fingertips. In other words, instead of worrying about the balance of moisture, what areas to weed next, border and security plans, and what plants grow better where—a raised bed is all of those facets and more in one box of organic delight.

Weed control is within reach for your whole garden here. Even with numerous beds, the psychological benefit of weeding eight different beds is both measurable and doable—versus having to weed a whole garden with rows and rows of plants staring you down. Pull up a stool and weed one box at a time with a whole lot less pain from kneeling or bending all day in a garden. Moreover, you won't need a rototiller either for raised beds. You'll even find this is actually a fairly inexpensive way to garden over time once the beds are in place.

Pull up a stool and weed one box at a time with a whole lot less pain from kneeling or bending all day in a garden.

Watering a raised bed is easy by installing a built-in (optional) irrigation system (some general insight on the items needed to make an at-home irrigation system is illustrated in Unit 4). The Director of Detail has tinkered enough with raised bed designs for several years now to render modifications from time to time. One of Jim's outcomes of quality improvement with the beds was to better understand water frequency as it correlates to water distribution.

Well, remember, we're talking about raised beds nourished from a few different traits of sustainability in a more controlled environment as compared to pulling out the hose and watering the back 40. In a raised bed, how deep and how level one waters is even more important as a result of its boxed growing perimeter. The good news is that determining the when and how a raised bed gets a drink of nature's cocktail is fairly programmable—leaving more time for bed-based gardeners to master the craft of growing with this medium.

Both foot critters and birds are less likely to visit your raised beds for a dining excursion because you can more easily assemble netting-related deterrents on the units. Covering a whole garden is time consuming and can become expensive. The wooded sides and smaller space to protect with a raised garden make maintaining a netting scheme rather simple. You can either affix netting to the sides of the beds or employ hoops to drape netting (described under the first *Beard's Behind-the-Blueprint Tips* on page 79). It's like taking ownership of your garden! Jim likes to call these growing systems, "weed and eat." Why not? You'll discover that's what you really do once they're in place!

For sake of do-it-yourself guidance in this chapter, we're going to focus on a common 3 ft., 6 inch by 7 ft. (4 by 8) raised garden bed. Again, the beauty of this concept is that you can make them almost any size or dimension to customize your green life—perhaps these instructions under a 3 ft., 6 inch by 7 ft. (4 by 8) model will serve as a foundation for doing just that!

Do-It-Yourself Steps to Making Raised Garden Beds

Once again, Jim is providing a guide for readers to tailor the design and construction of the growing systems presented in *Growing People: How green landscapes and growing spaces can change lives*. Have fun taking his foundational guidance and fine-tuning it to your liking.

Sample Dimension:

3.5 ft. by 7 ft. (+/-) by 12 inches high (+/-): Some gardeners like to make these beds higher than a foot as well—it all depends on each person's circumstances in regard to orthopedic considerations, aesthetics, space, and more.

For optimum growing and landscape balance, the length should always be twice as long as the width. Growers can customize any dimension that suits their preference.

Preferred Plants:

Vegetables, flowers, and herbs

Main Supplies:

Quantity (3), 8-ft. pieces of either rough sawn cedar or rough Douglas fir cedar (one of these will be cut in half and then you have a boxed perimeter for your raised bed)—these boards are 2 inches in width and 12 inches in height

Quantity (3), 4-ft. pieces of rough sawn cedar or rough Douglas fir cedar 2 by 4s to run across the inside width of the bed to keep it from bowing as a result of time and natural elements. Rest these pieces about 1.5 inches below the top of the bed. These boards also serve as a place to affix part of an optional irrigation system, which is generally outlined in Unit 4.

Titebond® 3 wood glue (good stuff to have handy for projects in this book)

Standard tapered drill for installing screws

A box of 3.5 inch DECKMATE® screws

The main frame of a traditional raised garden bed [26]

Beard's Behind-the-Blueprint Tip:

If you're planning to add hoops around your raised garden beds, use a 1-inch round PVC and (2) U brackets. Attach the PVC to the 12-inch sides with one-inch screws. Hoops provide opportunities to drape for a greenhouse effect or to deter critters and bugs, in addition to displaying or hanging garden art or plant baskets.

With our sample dimension, you can easily put up 4 hoops of equal spacing—running the length of the beds.

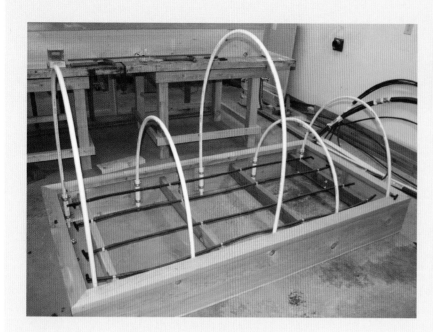

Beard's
Behind-the-Blueprint Tip:

For faster and easier assembly, pre-cut lumber and pre-drill all holes.

A traditional raised garden bed with hoops and irrigation system [27]

General Tips and Assembly Overview:

Pre-cut: (you'll need (3), 8-ft. pieces… two sides and two ends—the end pieces are from (1), 8 ft. piece cut in half under this sample dimension)

The ends are actually closer to 3 ft. by 8.5 inches

Pre-cut (3), 3-ft., 8.5 inch pieces to place equally inside the bed to serve the purpose of a reinforcement of the overall bed (keeping the frame intact).

Pre-drilling is required to prevent splitting during assembly.

1) Once the bed is framed, on the inside corners drive 2 by 2s into the ground to point of refusal to ensure that the bed is level and secure. A level box assures equal distribution of water and is aesthetically proportionate.

2) Place the reinforcement pieces 1.5 to 2 inches below the top of the raised bed on its interior.

3) Refer to the blueprint on page 81 for more details.

4) Fill raised bed with organic compost and a top dressing of worm castings… all about 1.5 to 2 inches below the top surface.

5) Water twice daily by hand or with the aid of a built-in irrigation system. A system like this has both programmable and solar capabilities, if desired (additional illustrations provided in Unit 4). Reduce to watering once daily when plants begin to mature.

Three traditional raised beds show off their bloom at Appleton Medical Center. [28]

Do-It-Yourself Steps to Making Raised Garden Beds *(continued)*

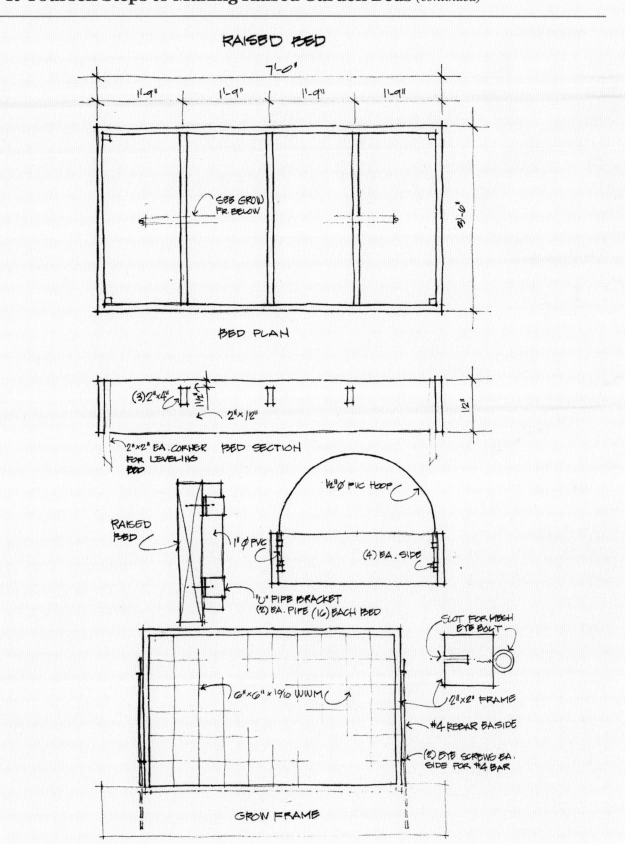

RAISED BED

7'-0"

1'-9" 1'-9" 1'-9" 1'-9"

3'-6"

SEE GROW
FR. BELOW

BED PLAN

(3) 2"x4"   1½"

2"x12"   12"

2"x2" EA. CORNER   BED SECTION
FOR LEVELING
BED

RAISED
BED

½"Ø PVC HOOP

1"Ø PVC

(4) EA. SIDE

"U" PIPE BRACKET
(2) EA. PIPE (16) EACH BED

SLOT FOR HIGH
EYE BOLT

6"x6"x10/10 WWM

2"x2" FRAME

#4 REBAR EA SIDE

(2) EYE SCREWS EA.
SIDE FOR #4 BAR

GROW FRAME

8 Straw Bale Fields Forever

Straw bale gardening is here to stay thanks to its low maintenance and mind-blowing results. Welcome to "soil-less" gardening for anywhere around your home, yard, or business.

On a deck or on the upstairs porch... in the grass or in a courtyard... along the house or alongside a patio... inside a rustic yard trailer or outside in the backyard... they are popping up everywhere and taking over the way to garden.

Straw bale gardens are becoming the talk of the town among the ranks of green growers in northeast Wisconsin. Already abundant in many areas around the Midwest, our little neck of the woods that is not big on change is just starting to catch on to this simple gardening technique. In fact, while putting the finishing narrative together for this book in August, Jim Beard was recently on regional TV segments and appeared in other media discussing the use of straw bales as emerging players in the world of sustainable gardening.

At a fundraiser in the mid-90s, I saw more hands in the air over a simple, everyday thing we might see a million times throughout a year and during holidays for sure. No words could explain the sight that was going down that day. I was part of an organizational entourage that coordinated the receiving end of a visit by Martha Stewart to the affluent and historic community of Kohler, Wisconsin.

Ms. Stewart was the headline presenter at a fall fundraiser in 1994 on the grounds at the gorgeous Woodlake Market—where she put on a craft and wreath-making demonstration. When it was done, she opened up the floor for questions from attendees.

Hundreds of hands covered the large indoor tent—it felt like the world's largest "high five" was happening. I briefly met Ms. Stewart prior to her speech and demo; it was clear that her passion toward the fundraising event was very genuine... a momentous moment in life.

A straw bale garden, seen here with a decorative cage, is a "soil-less" growing medium that can produce some mega plants. [29]

While one of Jim Beard's gigs was not quite at the level of Martha Stewart's occasion, the fixation on simple concepts between the two events were comparable. Granted, crafting and wreaths in general have stood the test of time when it comes to artistic, seasonal symbolism as they both relate to decorative flare. They bring an automatic touch to homes, businesses, and more. Yet, arguably their structural makeup is often created by the simplest of natural materials—twigs, vines, pine cones, branches, and an assortment of floral components usually anchored in wire. Like wreaths and many crafts, straw bales bear resemblance to said simplicity. They also have stood the test of time, but in a more agricultural impression.

Yes, hands flew in the air as energetically for Jim Beard as they did in Kohler some 20-plus years ago at the Martha Stewart event when it was time to field questions from his audience—there just weren't as many. On this day, Jim joined green thumb colleague Rob Zimmer for a fundraiser at Fox Valley Technical College before a hundred gardening enthusiasts in a small venue at the college's Appleton campus.

Garden Talk is an annual early spring event for the community set up to present the newest in green growing concepts for seasonal Wisconsinites. Attendees can get a jumpstart on their gardening plans each year by attending this space-limited function. Proceeds go to the FVTC Foundation's Seeds of Hope Fund—in place to help students in need of emergency assistance. Jim Beard has a roadie-like following for anything pertaining to growing plants and landscaping. This event exemplifies that type of following as many of the same people attend it annually, like witnessed at any number of his seasonal lectures across the region and state.

> Seeing a bale of straw on the floor and on the side of a room during this series of informative presentations caused a little chit chat throughout the morning among attendees.

One of Jim's first community events in which he introduced all of the *Beds, Bales, Buckets, and Brews* organic growing systems together in one public setting was at the 2015 Garden Talk. As much as garden beds (previous chapter), bucket beds (next chapter) and compost tea brewers (last chapter of this unit) raise eyebrows as to how they're made, a simple straw bale may have produced the most 180-degree head turns that morning. Seeing a bale of straw on the floor and on the side of a room during this series of informative presentations caused a little chit chat throughout the morning among attendees.

Why? In addition to straw bale gardens really not hitting stride yet in northeast Wisconsin, the mere appearance of a bale speculatively suggested something peculiar was in the air. This part of Wisconsin, albeit the third most populated region in the state, is fairly rich in agricultural activity. Naturally, straw bales are somewhat a regular sight around this area on farms, in the backs of trucks and flatbed trailers, and even around houses for a form of cheap insulation! Where they're not used to being seen is on back decks with plants growing out of them.

Straw bales offer very little aesthetic value on their own. Perceived as a bit cheap-looking and untidy around a house, they're value is found mostly on the farm for livestock bedding and some cattle feeding. So, imagine the looks of curiosity when Jim had one on the ground during Garden Talk. When Rob Zimmer's stellar talk on flowers, colors, and garden art concluded, Jim took the stage with *Beds, Bales, Buckets, and Brews*.

The moment of truth had arrived. What was up with the straw bale? Some folks in the audience likely knew about its relationship to growing by paying attention to industry magazines and news regarding straw bale growing on the rise in

This straw bale on wheels had a lot of people talking at the 2015 Garden Talk event at Fox Valley Technical College.

gardening. There appeared to be a large number of people, however, who were chomping at the bit to see what a simple straw bale was doing in the room. By the way… the event was held in FVTC's state-of-the-art Jones Dairy Farm Culinary Theatre. So, if you ever see straw on a menu around town somewhere let us know!

Jim says he feels more "at home" with himself these days since he's started to travel around and talk *Beds, Bales, Buckets, and Brews.* This is mostly because straw bales remind him of the blessings of his upbringing on a farm in northern Illinois with a hardworking family that had very little money. Lately more and more people are becoming interested in this book and his new organic growing systems (we call it the 4 Bs). Humbled, Jim would say, "I'm just a farm boy getting my hands dirty."

It's for certain those in attendance at Garden Talk were going to get their hands dirty after hearing Jim introduce a straw bale as the way to grow a garden. Repeat… "the way" to grow a garden—not just another way to grow a garden. He's serious about straw bales being the comprehensive way to grow seasonal vegetation without any soil. Their multi-faceted benefits are well experienced by those who've already worked with them:

- **Ergonomically friendly** – The average straw bale is between 18 and 24 inches high on its side, reducing the need for a lot of bending or sitting on knees. Many people with straw bale gardens just pull up a chair to plant, weed, or hang out by them! They are ideal for people with joint problems or those living with other physical disabilities. You could combine a straw bale gardening session with tea time. They could be garden tables of picturesque delight while we sip away a lazy afternoon.

- **Less labor-intense** – Straw bale gardening doesn't require the use of heavy equipment or most gardening tools, making it ideal for all ages and for those who can't lift a lot of weight. Most everything is done on top of the straw bale with minimal effort. Oh, what will you do with that extra space in your garden shed now without the rototiller and all those tools?

- **Everything is natural** – This is about as organic as it gets and no growing with soil! The bale and its energetic charge are all natural. A healthy straw bale (no mold, no darkness, a fresh smell accompanies a dry and crisp texture) is really a "soil-less" growing medium; hence, eliminating worries about soil quality or having to make multiple adjustments to grow in clay, sand, rock, etc. Goodbye, chemicals.

> A healthy straw bale is really a "soil-less" growing medium; hence, eliminating worries about soil quality or having to make multiple adjustments to grow in clay, sand, rock, etc. Goodbye, chemicals.

NOTE: For best results, use bales of either oats, wheat, rye, or barley origin. These bales don't contain many seeds, which aids in the stalks' ability to harbor a consistent, "soil-less" growing medium. Don't mistake straw for hay. Although some stalky hay could work for this type of gardening, most hay bales contain seeds, and grassy hay makes it difficult to bind root systems together because of a looser, less nutrient-based composition. Hay also has a solid center, whereas the middle of straw is hollower. That enables straw bales to hold more water.

- **Easy maintenance** – Very little weeding is required with straw bale gardening, and watering is a cinch because the root systems are isolated within their own healthy, vertical highway without competition from all directions as seen in soil gardening (nematodes, foreign bacteria, bugs, etc.). Straw bales make it a bit more difficult for four-legged critters to taste the good stuff as well since they'll have to do a little climbing as opposed to just eating along the way from one ground-level, soil garden to the next. If you make a rabbit work, it may move on to where the gettin' is a little easier.

- **A host to healthy organisms** – As straw bales begin to naturally transform into a growing medium, they are home to healthy organisms like mushrooms and purposeful worms. These organisms foster exceptional vegetable growth.

  NOTE: Frost is a bigger concern for plants growing in ground-level soil versus those in raised beds, bucket beds, or straw bales; however, gardeners should still exercise caution when frost and colder weather is prevalent in relation to beginning the growing process using straw bales or beds.

- **Portability** – Straw bales are relatively easy to move and maneuver in short distances. This adds creative options to your overall garden scheme of design and layout. Straw bales don't chew up a lot of space in your yard either. Hmmm… I think it looks better over there by the picnic table today. Go ahead and get creative!

- **Cost** – Rather than spending money on equipment and a lot of tools, straw bales are fairly inexpensive (or if you know a farmer or two, maybe next to nothing!). Excuse me, "How about an apple pie for a few straw bales?"

According to most industry research on straw bales, consumer-related (at-home) vegetable production commonly ranges anywhere from 20-25% percent higher in bales than when grown in soil. Most of this success is attributed to enhanced moisture and abundant oxygen available to the roots, producing extra warmth. The heat generated by decomposition provides a warmer growing environment that in turn speeds growth and allows planting two-four

weeks earlier than in soil. The established heat can also extend a growing process deeper into fall, if seasonality is an issue.

More on the heat factor in just a few paragraphs under Do-It-Yourself Steps because you want to control the heat of your bales prior to planting. Once planted, the heat source in the bales remains a natural boost to your plants, but too much heat can destroy roots.

Jim proclaims that one of the most enjoyable things about working with straw bales is that the mind runs rampant in terms of where to put them! Think of the possibilities on where a gardener can put these. When we talk about growing people, there is great potential in engaging kids in gardening through straw bale planting. They can learn how to grow plants out of the sides of the bales (referred to as running) and, of course, from the top, and then actually see the power of roots by way of rapid growth.

While finishing this book, Jim showed a few people around one of the greenhouses at Fox Valley Technical College a tomato plant root that actually grew out of the bottom of a straw bale within a few weeks. The sight of that root illustrates the health of this type of growing system.

Do-It-Yourself Steps to Straw Bale Gardening

Begin by gathering a healthy straw bale as characterized by the following:

A **healthy straw bale** (no mold, no dark colors, a fresh smell accompanies a dry and crisp texture) of either oats, wheat, rye, or barley origin. These bales typically don't contain any seeds, which aids in the stalks' ability to harbor a consistent, "soil-less" growing medium. Don't mistake straw for hay. Although some stalky hay could work for gardening, most hay bales contain seeds, and grassy hay makes it difficult to bind root systems together because of a looser, less nutrient composition.

Choose a **sunny location** to place your straw bale.

Turn the bale so that the narrow side with the cut straw (as opposed to straw that looks folded over) is **facing up**. The straw on the cut side of a bale looks shorter and consistent in regard to length and it feels sharper. Folded over straw looks combed and uneven, as well as softer to the touch because you're not feeling ends that were cut during baling.

You may place one bale next to one another, but it's advisable to **leave enough room in between the rows** to easily access plants.

Plant considerations:

Almost anything that grows in ground soil will bloom in a bale of straw. Exceptions are tall plants such as indeterminate tomatoes and corn, as well as vine-heavy vegetation that likes to "run" for great distances.

Tomatoes grow successfully in straw bales, but the key is to use determinate varieties. Other common plants that grow from straw bales in this region include **squash, peppers, cucumbers, radishes, carrots, parsley, kale,** and **flowers** galore!

Try planting (running) squash and flowers on the side after you master the tops of the bales. You'll have people stopping in their tracks… pretty wild.

Conditioning your bale before planting:

- QUALIFIER: Conditioning (or charging) straw bales to prepare them for growing is a non-scientific process not synonymous to any one method for either professional or amateur gardeners. Results are subjective based on continuous improvements and customization to preference.

The following steps are presented as a hypothesis based on effective growing results from numerous gardeners, both professional and amateur. Jim recommends that the straw bale growing process be adjusted to fit the customized needs of each grower, professional or amateur.

Have you ever seen mist come out of a pile of horse manure if it's raked or shoveled? If you're into organic gardening, have you ever felt a sense of energy coming from inside a compost pile while working around it? The heat is on, isn't it? We're talking hot—like potentially up to 200 degrees. Natural growing dynamics rely on heat for best results, but it must be controlled. Straw bales work off of the same concept. **Conditioning** a straw bale for planting is essentially speeding up its decomposition to reduce overall heat. Skipping this critical step can destroy plant roots.

Do-It-Yourself Steps to Straw Bale Gardening *(continued)*

Conditioning, or charging, is a fundamental step in growing plants with straw bales. [30]

The process of conditioning a straw bale usually takes about 10-14 days. A conditioned bale after that time should appear very black on top and feel soft in the middle. Before planting, we must lower the temperature in our straw bale to below 80 degrees. To get there, let's begin with the following timeline to serve as a guide to **Conditioning**:

DAY 1: Poke shallow slits (about 1-2 inches deep) along the top of the bale with the end of a garden trowel. Mix up the angles when poking and create enough slits that they outnumber the "non-slit space" atop the bale.

Soak the bale thoroughly with water and then spread 4 cups of generic compost over the holes (NOTE: Jim uses a proprietary compost, but a generic compost should work).

DAY 2: Soak the bale.

Record temperature from the center of the bale on top. A large meat thermometer will suffice.

DAY 3: Soak the bale. Record temperature.

DAY 4: Spread 4 cups of worm castings and 4 cups of generic compost over the top of the bale. Soak the bale.

DAY 5: Soak the bale. Record temperature.

DAY 6: Soak the bale. Record temperature.

DAY 7: Spread 4 cups of worm castings and 4 cups of generic compost over the top of the bale. Soak the bale.

DAY 8: Soak the bale. Record temperature.

DAY 9: Soak the bale. Record temperature.

DAY 10: Spread 4 cups of worm castings and 4 cups of generic compost over the top of the bale. Soak the bale.

DAY 11: Soak the bale. Record temperature.

DAY 12: Soak the bale. Record temperature.

DAY 13: Plant IF the temperature of the bale is below 80 degrees! Soak after planting.

For that matter, as soon as the temperature is below 80 degrees... start planting at any time during the conditioning process.

If the bale's temperature is still slightly above 80 degrees, repeat the process starting at DAY 10. Try the process with another bale all over again if the temperature is above 95 degrees after a couple more days under this model.

Again, results will vary. Some growers will see temperatures as low as the 60s after just 10 days; others will take a bit longer to realize heat reduction. Plant about two-three plants per bale from the top and one-two plants on the side if you desire a running technique.

Watering schedule:

Built-in irrigation, which was introduced in the previous chapter for raised garden beds, is recommended, but not necessary. Such an irrigation method depends on investing time up front and the individual preference of each gardener. As mentioned, pipe irrigation beelines moisture to the root system more effectively than traditional water that freely flows from above plants via a hose or watering can.

Moderately water daily for the first week, twice a day—early a.m. and early p.m. Avoid watering between 1:00 and 4:00 p.m. Follow this routine until germination.

At germination, moderately water once daily until harvest.

Optional screened boxes:

To add a little rustic-style splendor to your straw bales, place them in screened boxes—a Jim Beard original! Some can even come with wheels on them. We've seen bookmobiles, ice cream trucks, and mobile barbecue restaurants and more—now we're welcoming a garden on wheels coming to a farmer's market near you! What next?

Screened boxes around straw bale gardens are gaining steam. Jim's good friend, garden expert, and provider of the Welcome in our book, Melinda Myers, highlighted them during her botanical presentations at the 2015 Wisconsin State Fair.

Jim is still mastering his craft with the decorative screened boxes for straw bales; therefore, they were not included in the book as a do-it-yourself project. The Director of Detail did furnish a few sketches at the end of this chapter as supplementary content.

Please refer to the Inquiries section on page 141 on how you can obtain further information about this product.

General maintenance:

Pull a few weeds and watch your plants grow! At the end of the growing season, pull your plants and use the same bale for one more year. Plant potatoes next year by following the same steps as outlined in DAYS 1 thru 13.

After year two, use the straw bale as garden mulch and see your nearest farmer for some new ones.

Beard's Behind-the-Blueprint Tip:

Jim recommends Joel Karsten's book, **Straw Bale Gardens: The Breakthrough Method for Growing Vegetables Anywhere, Earlier and with No Weeding!** *(Quayside Publishing's Cool Springs Press, 2013) for a more in-depth look at straw bale gardening.*

Do-It-Yourself Steps to Straw Bale Gardening *(continued)*

Beard's Behind-the-Blueprint Tip:

The Director of Detail dishes out these sketches on straw bale gardening and decorative screened boxes as supplementary content:

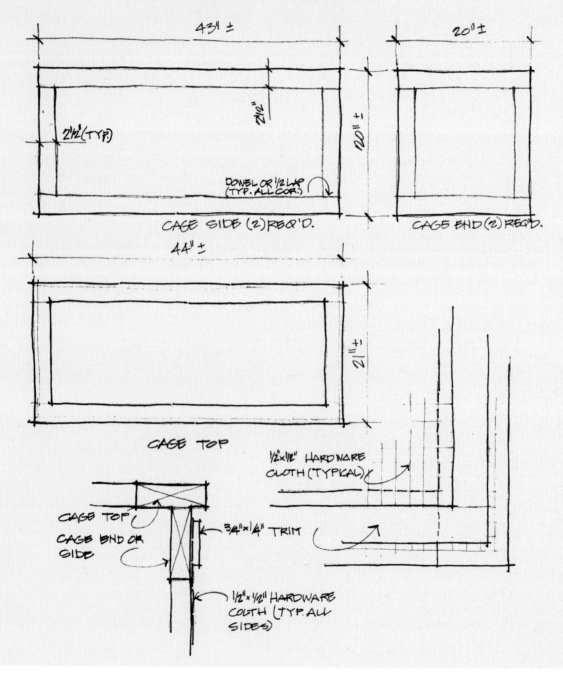

STRAW BALE CAGE (OPTIONAL)

9 A Crop in the Bucket

A few circles on top of a table and an ergonomically-friendly garden is yours. Raised bucket benches invite you to once again pull up a chair and garden away at a green desk under the sun.

People were crowding by the booth for what appeared to be a bean bag toss game. Now bean bag tosses are everywhere in Wisconsin as a form of outdoor seasonal leisure. Think about it… what goes with beer, brats, and a ball game at Lambeau Field, Camp Randall Stadium, Miller Park, or numerous other college and university stadiums in the Badger state? You got it—recreation.

Enter bean bag tosses. In this state, tailgating is a cultural expectation when going to outdoor athletic events. You can't walk from your vehicle to a stadium without seeing parking lanes of bean bags flying in the air landing atop homemade structures with all kinds of logos, colors, and designs. The holes in which the bean bags slip through come in numerous shapes and sizes as well, but typically they're circular.

Yes, it's all fun and games before kickoff, but a bean bag toss at an outdoor garden expo? Maybe. There's got to be something for kids to do (even though it is big kids playing this game at tailgate parties) at spring garden shows while grownups drool over what's new and what's desired for the upcoming growing season.

The twist here is that the booth I was approaching at the 2014 Garden Fair in early June at the Green Bay Botanical Garden was Jim Beard's. Jim must've had something up his sleeve to transform the booth he was running for Fox Valley Technical College (FVTC) into a bean bag event. If a bean bag toss was going down, you can bet it was going to be fun with Jim at the helm.

My intention at his booth was to grab a few photos on this Saturday morning. Jim was once

A raised bucket bench garden typically consists of three-to-six buckets, depending on the dimension of the table, size of the buckets, and individual preference.

again representing the college simply because he loves what he does. He gets to meet new people and share with them what's going on educationally in the areas of landscape construction and horticulture at FVTC. That's Jim, 24/7/365.

My curiosity piqued while approaching Jim as about 10-15 people surrounded his booth. All I could see was a table with a few holes in it near the back of his booth. His visitors were marveling at it and/or something else as I neared the gathering. I didn't see any bean bags flying through the air, but his structure certainly brought that depiction to mind. Upon arrival to his booth, Jim greeted me and continued to highlight a table with holes in it for his visitors.

Maybe Jim needed sleep—after all, this was day two of three in some late spring heat and humidity

that would consume 30-plus hours of his time once the event was said and done. Maybe the heat got to him and he simply made a mistake with his table because there were holes in it! We are all prone to do weird stuff when overtired, right? Whatever was the case at this moment by his booth, it was an attention grabber!

Jim's alleged bean bag table was pure white with three holes in it. Most bean bag tables are on the ground in an angled position, kind of like a low park or water slide for young children, but Jim's was balanced and elevated. There were no logos or sports designs on his table. All right—kidding aside now as I admittedly could figure out the structure the closer I got to it. A little Wisconsin culture from time to time keeps us grounded, and for Jim, any "structure" is worth taking a deeper look at. Chalk up another structure for Jim… green bean bag toss tables to hit the market soon? You never know.

Thus far in *Growing People: How green landscapes and garden spaces can change lives*, Jim has revealed how personalized, organic gardens of the elevated variety can bring orthopedic preservation to our joints, healthier vegetation to our bodies, and simplicity to our green thumbs. Raised bucket benches, or green (sustainable) desks under the sun as we playfully sometimes refer to them, now join that line of advantageous growing systems.

Growing Mobility

Jim's raised bucket benches introduce an almost seamless style of gardening with respect to individual mobility. The model brings to mind walking up and down a greenhouse. While visiting your favorite retail greenhouse, how often do you actually bend? Plants are basically propped up on long tables or on a series of benches for optimum browsing pleasure. Yes, sometimes we'll bend to grab a plant on the floor that may look nice, but for the most part, we walk up and down aisles of green while perusing at most

Garden enthusiasts annually attend Jim's booth at the Garden Fair in Green Bay to see what he's highlighting for the growing season.

plant stations. When it's time to purchase a plant or two, we reach, grab, and go. When your plants are ripe at home using a raised bucket bench, the same effortless process occurs when picking these gems off the vine.

For employees who work at greenhouses and plant stations alike, the raised tables make watering and other light plant maintenance a breeze. When plants require irrigation or some weeding at home, an effortless process can occur in your backyard as well by way of a raised bucket bench.

In addition, a customized irrigation system that is also optionally programmable can take care of watering plants on any number of Jim's growing systems while you're off doing something else. These automated watering systems use emitters and piping that is nearly invisible among the fast-growing greens in whatever bed or bale contraption suits your fancy. Unit 4 in this book illustrates some general irrigation concepts and related parts if you're inclined to explore that supplemental option.

Growing Simplicity

For gardeners, raised bucket benches provide start-to-finish simplicity. From assembly of the table to blending a natural growing medium in everyday buckets… to planting… to watching bloom—these furnishings of foliage are contagiously fun in both construction and leisure. Imagine rows of raised bucket benches in whatever placement scheme is desired in your backyard or around the house.

With these systems, gardeners can slowly see the plants fill (and essentially cover up) or take over the table top space during a growing process. This is what Jim refers to as "watching bloom." It won't happen as much with more vertical-growing plants, but the concept of watching plants grow out of nothing (so it appears) is pretty cool.

Pull up a chair once again—raised bucket bench gardening joins our lineup of easy growing systems. The most you'll ever do is bend minimally to play in the bucket soil or pull a weed or two. Sitting with your knees under a bench like at the office, for instance, is a pretty comfortable way to garden versus constant bending or kneeling. Moreover, where else can you find an up close view of your plants like this without slithering through a jungle? Sitting on a chair and leaning over the bench gives a gardener a front row ticket to leaves, stems, fruit, soil, irrigation, and anything else at ground level—without being on the ground!

Do-It-Yourself Steps to Bucket Bench Construction

This section refers to a three-hole bucket bench with identical openings using empty five-gallon buckets (with exterior rings near the top) as our sample. Our sample height is 21 inches off the ground. The five-gallon buckets will reside securely in the holes by way of some friction and their top exterior rings (serving as a grasp, resting on top of the plywood above the circles). Jim says that another popular option to the bench is a five-bucket configuration, comprised of three, five-gallon buckets and two, two-gallon buckets (as shown on page 93).

1) Begin with a 3/4 inch piece of non-treated plywood, 2 by 4 ft. in length. Also supply yourself with three pieces of 3/4-inch rough sawn cedar, which is known as a 1 by 4 by 8, as well as (1), 8 by 2 by 2 cedar board (used for the legs of your table).

NOTE: You can customize the height and essentially the size of your table. For this sample, again, we're going with three holes on top for three buckets and 21 inches off the ground for height. At the time this book was nearing publication, Jim was busy at work making a higher and wider raised garden bench for some amazing people with cerebral palsy—can't write fast enough with this guy in terms of growing people.

Five pieces of wood are all you need to make a three-hole bucket bench. You will first work with the plywood until Step 5.

2) Space the three holes before cutting them equally across the 2 by 4 ft. piece of plywood. You should be about 5 inches in from the side,

Beard's Behind-the-Blueprint Tip:

Next, we'll be cutting three holes on top of a secured piece of plywood that is laid balanced on four corners with sawhorses and clamped in place for safety. Before we do so, it is important to measure the diameter of the buckets.

Not all buckets will be exactly the same diameter based on brand. A five-gallon bucket will be about 11 inches in diameter.

running the length of the board for the first hole (5 inches in, then about 11 inches wide for the first circle accounts for about 16 inches of the board's total length of 48 inches… 16 times 3 puts us right where we need to be for equal spacing, length wise).

For width spacing, it's recommended to place two holes near to the top of the board and the third one, positioned in the middle between the two, should dip lower. The two top circles should begin about 4 inches from the top, and the middle circle should begin about 4 inches from the bottom of the board.

These markings signify the very far edge of a circle (length) and the very top point of a circle (width) from their respective sides (in a length and width context considering the entire piece of plywood).

3) Use a router with a compass attachment to determine circumference down to the 16th of an inch. If you can't access a router with attached compass, no problem. You can use a hand compass to sketch a circle.

Drill a hole first before using the sabre saw to cut the circles. When turned off, the saw blade should be able to rest in the drilled hole first. Then slowly and carefully follow the compass line around the circle to cut open each hole for the buckets.

Carefully cut the three holes.

4) Paint both sides of the plywood, including the exposed inner wood resulting from the cuts, to reduce delamination and warping as the board will take on moisture. Use two coats of KILS® primer, followed by one coat of a latex enamel of choice. Allow time to dry thoroughly before any further assembly.

5) Cut a piece of 3/4 inch rough sawn cedar using a table saw into two pieces, 4 ft. in length (cut the board in half) to serve as the **exterior skirt** on the longer sides of the bench. The skirt helps bond the bench together as a whole unit.

6) Cut another 3/4 inch rough sawn cedar piece into two pieces that are 3 ft., 9 inches in length to serve as the longer sides of the **interior skirt** of the bench. These pieces will help secure the legs of the bench in a snug manner. Clamp legs to the **exterior skirt** and cut to fit the inside 1 by 4 as a "friction fit."

7) Cut the third piece of 3/4 inch rough sawn cedar into 2 pieces that will serve as the width boards of the **exterior skirt** and measure about 25.5 inches on each side, plus or minus a fraction—so with your overall wood supply, size to fit.

21-inch pieces make up the under plywood **interior skirt** on the width ends, designed to work in harmony with all **interior skirt** pieces to provide a snug "friction fit" for the legs. More on that in just a bit.

NOTE: The width of your exterior and interior skirt boards should be set to go at 3.5 inches from buying 1 by 4 by 8s. For whatever reason due to variance in wood brands that your width is not 3.5 inches, either check this measurement during your pre-purchasing of the wood or simply customize your bench to personal liking.

8) Turn the table upside down and begin working from underneath at this point.

9) Glue (using Titebond® 3 wood glue) the newly-cut cedar (3.5 inch-wide pieces) around the outside of the now-dried (from the paint) plywood for an **exterior skirt**.

Beard's Behind-the-Blueprint Tip:

For added strength to the bench, drill three small evenly-spaced holes across each of the skirt boards. Drill small screws (#6 or #8) in each hole to the plywood. The length of the screws should always be twice as long as the thickness of the wood.

10) Cut the 8 ft., 2 by 2 cedar into legs. For this model, cut them about 20.25 inches high (the remaining 3/4 inch will compensate for the amount of space the plywood consumes—giving your table a total height of 21 inches). Your corner spaces as you look at them with the table upside down will be two inches in square diameter.

Once your exterior skirt is in place and you have allowed some time for the glue to dry, now direct your attention to the interior skirt.

Do-It-Yourself Steps to Bucket Bench Construction *(continued)*

11) Using 8 wood clamps, clamp each leg in place from both the end and from the side (from the direction of the length and from the direction of the width). Basically, you're clamping at two points in each corner where the interior skirt will be assembled momentarily. This is an important step. Your table needs to have an effective "friction fit" (or field fit) that snugly holds the legs in place for both durability and stability when gardening.

Beard's Behind-the-Blueprint Tip:

Jim designed the bucket benches to have a "friction fit" so storing them at the end of a growing season is a cinch. While gardening, gravity holds them in place supported by the weight of soil and plants in the buckets. When removing the buckets at the end of the season, just turn over the table and slide out the legs. Then store your table upright as opposed to length wise to save space. Don't forget to store the legs together as well when the time comes, along with a simple stacking of buckets! Now, back to our regularly-scheduled broadcast of finishing up this innovative garden!

The interior skirt under the bucket bench forms space to support the four legs of the table while adding durability to its overall foundation.

The four legs of the bucket bench (table) are designed as "friction fit."

It's time to make the **interior skirt**. This part of the bench is comprised of the 4, shorter cedar pieces you cut in STEP 7. The 4 pieces will be attached to the underside of the plywood and assume "friction fit" roles to keep the legs of the table snugly in place in each corner.

Do-It-Yourself Steps to Bucket Bench Construction *(continued)*

Keep your table upside down and proceed as follows:

12) Glue (using Titebond® 3 wood glue) on the narrow side of the newly-cut 4 pieces of cedar for the interior skirt to be affixed under the plywood (again, from an upside down view).

13) Remove clamps without disturbing position of legs.

14) Attach 4 **interior skirt** cedar boards against plywood and snug to each leg. Allow time to dry.

Beard's Behind-the-Blueprint Tip:

Once the bench is complete and just before planting, carefully drill two additional small screws on the interior boards where they touch the exterior pieces for added durability. It is best practice to enlist the help of another person to provide resistance on the other side of the exterior boards… of course, safely and away from your drill points.

Gluing and clamping help bond the interior skirt to the exterior frame and create a "friction fit" system.

15) Clamp from the outside of the **exterior skirt** to the **interior skirt** this time for an hour.

16) Remove clamps. Your bench legs should rub against the interior skirt when put in place for best results. Again, during your construction, keep in mind the importance of a "friction fit" when it comes to your bench legs.

17) With the assistance of another person, carefully turn the table over with fingers holding the legs in place. You are now ready to begin gardening on a bench!

18) Drill a half-inch hole in the center and at the bottom of each bucket (make sure to clean and rinse whatever substance was in there before it became empty) and then insert the buckets into the holes. They, too, should slide in somewhat like a "friction fit" as well if the holes were cut properly. The bucket rings should catch the plywood and rest accordingly in the holes.

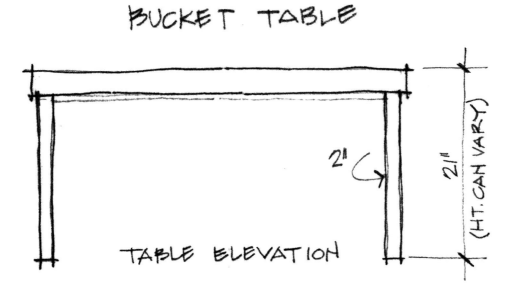

BUCKET TABLE

TABLE ELEVATION

2"

21" (HT. CAN VARY)

Do-It-Yourself Steps to Bucket Bench Construction *(continued)*

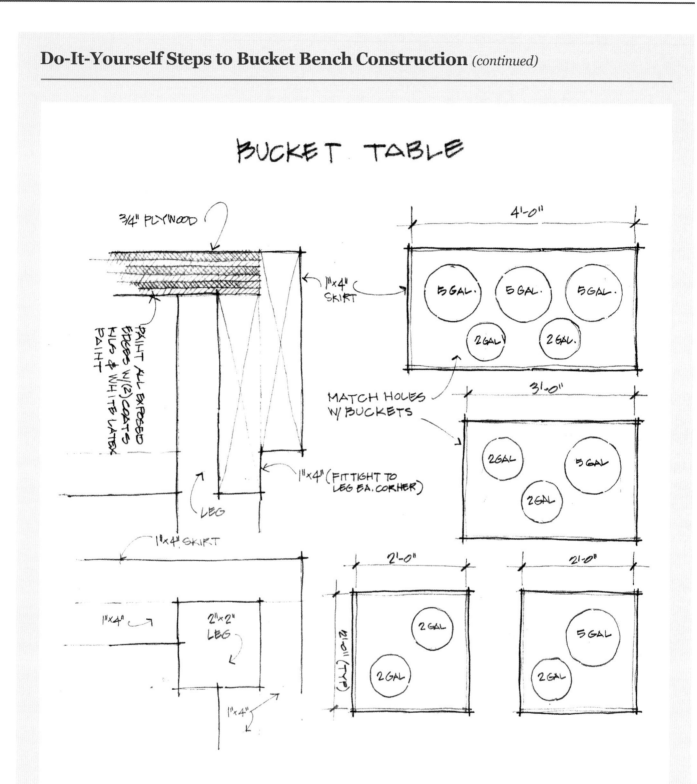

BUCKET TABLE

Do-It-Yourself Steps to Bucket Bench Gardening

With your three- or five-hole bucket bench ready for action, let's grow!

1) Once the buckets are firmly intact in their holes, place a piece of Typar® landscape fabric about 3 inches square over the center of each bucket at the bottom where the half inch hole resides. This enhances drainage during the plant-growing process.

2) Place an inch of washed pea gravel in the bottom of each bucket so it rides to an equal level around the diameter.

3) Place an identical piece of Typar® landscape fabric on top of the pea gravel to fit lightly all around the bucket.

4) Fill each bucket with compost-based soil to about an inch from the top. Compost and worm castings mixed together is Jim's favorite, but any organic medium will suffice—again, it boils down to individual preference.

Beard's Behind-the-Blueprint Tip:

The gravel and fabric under the soil serve as a sink. Such a set up allows for optimum drainage versus having soil run to the bottom of the bucket, where moisture can build up along the edges and cause growing disorders.

5) Plant! Tomatoes, peppers, and salad onions are great in this system. Herbs grow well, too, but smaller buckets are recommended for them. With tomatoes, use metal rings and bend them at the bottom just a bit and position their ends to touch the sides of the buckets as you insert them downward into the soil. Now you have an ideal supportive growing device in place for vertical growth!

Five-gallon buckets virtually held in the air with drainage systems are coming into their own as gardens. We'll have to think of something to do with the handles! Knowing Jim, he will.

Raised bucket benches and straw bale gardens together make a green-thumb getaway.

10 Botanical Brewer

The results are indisputable when plants absorb natural nourishment. Leave the chemicals at the store and make a green impression by brewing your own compost tea.

NOTE: Compost tea is for plant use only and NOT for human consumption.

"What the heck could be growing out of that large pile of horse manure?" That was just another random question for Jim Beard while he consulted with my wife, Kim, and I about some general landscaping around the house. We had noticed vegetation coming up from such a pile on our neighbor's property. "Pumpkins, most likely," Jim replied.

We had to see this to believe it. After a couple of weeks, Kim and I revisited the pile to see if horses and Halloween really had something in common! They sure do. Big orange beauties were growing straight out of horse droppings, and they were the best-looking pumpkins we had ever seen.

After our little field trip to the neighbor's manure pile and being horse owners ourselves, please take what's about to be said with genuine truth: "Compost is unbelievably fascinating." OK, we don't spend our free time watching paint dry either—but we love to learn just like you!

More people are beginning to make composting a part of their growing repertoire. Some folks go all out and make compost piles (lots of stuff goes in there); others, like Kim and I, just try to incorporate organic goodness into our lives whenever possible. If pumpkins can grow out of horse manure, what else? We can attest that a little aged (one-two years) horse manure has done wonders to young blue spruce trees.

If you don't know a cowboy or cowgirl to access horse manure or perhaps don't have enough space to develop a compost pile, how about brewing some green nutrition for your plants (now that you have three new organic growing systems in place thanks to Jim!)? Yes, you can become a brew master for many things green.

Before we embark upon brewing compost tea, here are some advantages from switching to natural fertilization over toxic chemicals. After all, compost is the single most important supplement for your soil (and even in straw bales as a "soil less" growing medium).

An at-home tea brewer (for plants) really takes the force of churning and couples it with a constant injection of air to develop outstanding compost.

Compost:

- Adds humus—the heart and soul of healthy soil, comprised of material that results from the decay of organic matter.

- Is virtually free, easy to make in whatever form you desire, and beneficial to the environment.

- Can reduce considerable amounts of household and institutional waste. Most landfills in North America are near capacity and many are closed down permanently. A more concerted effort is underway to fill landfills with compostable materials, but that transformation must begin at home and at work.

- Ushers useful micro-organisms into the soil for both aeration and decomposition of organic elements, reducing the chance for plant disease.

Do-It-Yourself Steps to Brewing Compost Tea

Again, an at-home compost tea brewing system is another contraption that opens the door for customization in design and functionality. Jim believes in giving people a baseline of know-how with room for personal modification. That's why students and attendees of his lectures come back for more… there is so much potential for tweaking, tinkering, and creating based off of one successful model. It's simply fun whenever you can put your personal stamp on something. He truly wants you to do just that with all of these growing concepts.

Compost tea brewers provide an advantageously-confined medium to continuously add air in a setting where organic biology explodes. That explosion, in turn, multiplies microbes from the organic compost—building a rich, potent formula for liquid plant nutrition. An at-home tea brewer (for plants) really takes the force of churning and couples it with a constant injection of air to develop outstanding compost.

Jim is going to present the easiest compost tea brewer and then one that was done by his good friend, Steve Finley, from the Preface of *Growing People: How green landscapes and garden spaces can change lives.* Steve is also one of Jim's business partners for a company named, JANDS and a trusted industry colleague. These two are revolutionizing the way growers use their soil—from the smallest of backyards to huge farm fields.

Finally, Jim, as only the Director of Detail can, will provide some optional alterations to your brewer in this chapter, if desired. He has an abundance of experience in making at-home compost tea brewing systems for plants—ones that have been successfully replicated by students and members of the community from attending his classes and lectures.

NOTE: The illustrations in this chapter DO NOT reflect the actual amount of water needed to effectively and safely conduct an at-home compost tea brewing system. A limited amount of water was used in brewing buckets for visual purposes ONLY for readers to see devices in a submersible manner, in addition to a general overview of their operational functionality.

Do-It-Yourself Steps to Brewing Compost Tea *(continued)*

THE BASIC BREWER

Gather the following items:

A clean empty **5-gallon paint bucket** with cap on lid to function as your brewing station—retain the lid

A **mesh bag** (similar to a sieve for pools or aquariums) or a **nylon** to serve as a "sock" that will hold biology inside the bucket during the brewing process. Either the bag or nylon should be about 7 to 10 inches in length.

Easy access to well or natural **water** (or pretreat chlorinated water as described on the next page).

A small EcoPlus® **air stone** with ¼-inch or ½-inch tube to attach to an EcoPlus® **air pump** (Model # 728450 as shown)

2 cups of worm castings and/or fungal compost as a biology charge

A **circle saw** (for cutting plastics) to cut a 3.5-inch hole on the bucket lid, located opposite the side of the cap

A standard extension cord (length needed depends on your setting)

Beard's Behind-the-Blueprint Tip:

In this industry like many others, relationships are an integral part of the success of your growing systems and plants. Jim recommends using certain brand-name products and suppliers of organic materials throughout his lectures and classroom instruction, in addition to steps and references in this book. He attributes much of his achievements to several years of working with different brand products and finding ones that produce the best results. Diverting from Jim's recommendations is your prerogative; he is simply sharing his experience and supplying guidance.

An air stone is commonly used for a basic compost brewing system.

Follow these steps to make a BASIC BREWER:

NOTE: The following concoction is designed to cover about a 1,000 square feet of garden space per 1 gallon of water. Brew to desired strength. You can't over apply compost tea, but strive for consistency.

1) While exercising caution, carefully cut a hole in the top of the bucket lid, measuring about 3.5 inches in diameter and located on the opposite side of the cap (these caps are close to the edge of the buckets). This larger hole will function as the opening in which you will place the mesh bag or nylon sock filled with worm castings.

2) While exercising caution, cut or poke a hole about a 1/2 inch in diameter in the middle of the cap so the air stone cord fits through the opening with ample slack (use a strong tool that will not slip while poking or hammering downward).

3) Fill the bucket 3/4 full of well or natural water.

Beard's Behind-the-Blueprint Tip:

If filling with city water or highly-chlorinated H₂O, begin your brewing process with STEP 11. It's advisable in this case to aerate and churn your water for 2 hours before brewing compost tea. This preliminary step, which is done before you put in any worm castings or compost in the bucket, is done to rid the chlorine through infusing air into the water. Chlorine will otherwise destroy your natural biology.

After 2 hours of dechlorination, resume with STEP 4.

4) Place the lid securely on top of the bucket.

5) Gently drop the air stone to the bottom of the bucket. Run the top of its cord (tube end) upward through the small hole made in STEP 2 from inside the bucket.

6) Once through the hole and atop the lid of the bucket, attach the tube at the end of the air stone into the connector of the air pump.

7) Rest the air pump balanced on top of the lid.

8) Fill the mesh bag or nylon sock with 2 cups of worm castings and/or compost of choice.

Beard's Behind-the-Blueprint Tip:

In place of worm castings or to add to a mix with worm castings (still keeping the total measurement to 2 cups), Jim recommends Purple Cow® as a retail brand of compost. You can also add your own compost, if desired.

9) Insert the filled mesh bag or nylon sock into the 3.5-inch manufactured hole so it rests about half way down the bucket (NEVER rest this item at the bottom of the bucket).

10) Clamp the top of the filled mesh bag or nylon sock to desired preference using either small clamps or another fit arrangement. It's important that the bag or sock remain secured for the entire brewing process in which the bucket will be vibrating constantly from the movement of the electric air pump.

11) Plug your air pump into a standard wall socket to give it power.

12) Brew for 8-24 hours. Your at-home BASIC BREWER is adding oxygen to the compost mix which explodes the biology into making more nutrition.

Do-It-Yourself Steps to Brewing Compost Tea *(continued)*

THE BASIC BREWER (continued)

> #### Beard's Behind-the-Blueprint Tip:
>
> *Since an ideal brew takes at least 8 hours, consider the time of day you're going to begin the process. Compost tea should be applied immediately to your plants after brewing or it becomes anaerobic and loses nutrients. DO NOT apply between 1:00 and 4:00 in the afternoon.*

Jim underscores this is a BREW & APPLY *immediately* activity!

13) After 8 hours, turn off power to the air pump.

14) Detach the tube end of the air stone from air pump.

15) Slide detached tube end of the air pump under the small hole on the cap. Remove the lid of the bucket.

16) Remove the air stone.

17) Using a funnel, pour compost tea into desired containers for distribution of fertilization.

18) Apply compost tea generously near the stems of your smaller plants and around a larger perimeter with trees and bigger foliage. Jim likes to remind us that when we're out for dinner, the stem of the wine glass is the trunk of a tree, but the dinner plate is the perimeter of its root system. Ongoing research suggests that the serving tray that was used to deliver the plate to your table is the actual root system of most trees. Be generous.

Compost tea is great fertilizer for lawns as well!

> #### Beard's Behind-the-Blueprint Tip:
>
> *In the early part of the growing season, apply compost tea in your raised beds and straw bales twice a week—even right after planting seeds. Reduce to weekly in summer.*
>
> *If treating annuals, add 1 tablespoon of non-sulfurous molasses to the compost tea mix of worm castings. For perennials, add 1 tablespoon of oat or rice flour to the compost tea mix of worm castings. If treating both together within the same tight growing space, add both to the compost mix of worm castings.*

19) Rinse all fertilizer containers. It is best practice to use the same containers all the time for compost tea distribution and not inter-mix them with other ingredients.

20) Fill 5-gallon brew bucket with a half-gallon of water and a quarter cup of hydrogen peroxide. Reassemble all units from STEPS 4 through 11, EXCLUDING STEPS 8-10 because we're cleaning the unit now, not brewing.

21) Run air pump for a half hour to allow for the churning of the water, air infusions, and hydrogen peroxide to clean the bottom portion of the bucket. Then scrub the remainder of both the air stone and the bucket by hand using the available

water and hydrogen peroxide in the bucket. Make sure you scrub the air stone thoroughly with a rigorous rinse.

22) Clean mesh bag or discard nylon sock.

23) Store parts in a box or designated area to prevent damage and turn bucket upside down until next use.

FINLEY'S
FERMENTED FERTILIZER

Steve applies the following modifications for a bit of an amended brewing experience, if desired:

NOTE: There are no air stones used in this brewing system, reducing the amount of clean up time after each brew.

- PVC pipe (3/4 inch) runs from the air pump instead of a cord from an air stone, creating a stronger churn and air infusion into the brewing process.

- Use the same hole cuts as found on the BASIC BREWER, but with FINLEY'S FERMENTED FERTILIZER... the smaller hole on the cap is used to connect to the air pump and to run PVC into the bucket. A small clear tube is used to slide snugly into the air pump receiver.

At the end of the contraption is a horizontal handle bar device that serves as a churner at the bottom of the bucket.

The larger hole on FINLEY'S FERMENTED FERTILIZER is used to hold a mesh bag or nylon sock in place, just like as seen on a BASIC BREWER.

- Cut and assemble PVC to fit using 3/4-inch PVC elbows, T insertions, and nipples (2 inches long).

- Cut small slits at the ends of each of the 2 caps, which are used at the ends of the handle bar churners to optimize air injection into the brew.

The top view of Steve's compost brewing system

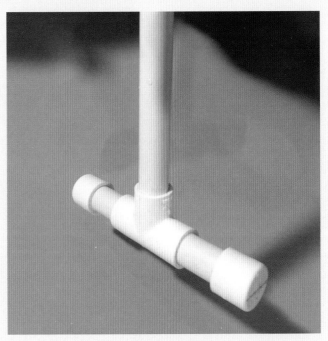

The churning device at the bottom of Steve's compost brewing system covers a broad diameter.

Do-It-Yourself Steps to Brewing Compost Tea *(continued)*

<table>
<tr>
<td>

FINLEY'S FERMENTED FERTILIZER (continued)

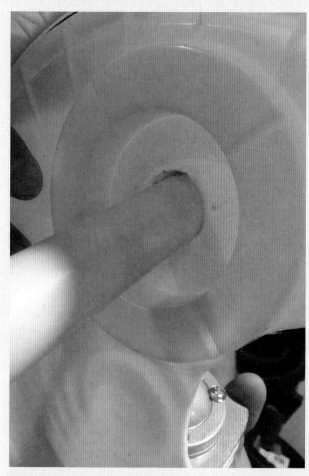

The view of underside piping on Steve's compost brewing system runs downward from the small hole on the cap.

Again, custom construct to fit. When done applying the compost tea to plants, the only necessary cleanup is to run a half-gallon of water with a quarter cup of hydrogen peroxide as if you were repeating the brewing process for a half hour. Scrub clean any PVC or part of the bucket as needed after the cleanup brewing process concludes. Clean and store parts accordingly.

</td>
<td>

BEARD'S BREWER

Jim applies the following modifications to offer another version of an at-home compost tea brewing system for plants:

NOTE: There are no air stones used in this brewing system, reducing the amount of clean up time after each brew.

- This brewer does not require a bucket lid. The top of the bucket is open.
- Some soldering is required for assembly with Jim's model.
- Rigid copper piping (1/2 inch with threaded fittings) is used for 4 main purposes with this brewer:

1. It connects to the air pump using a vinyl air hose (about 1/4 inch to 3/8 inch). Make sure there is an adjacent bench or small table to rest the air pump on next to the bucket.

Copper piping and a lidless appearance characterize Jim's compost brewing system.

</td>
</tr>
</table>

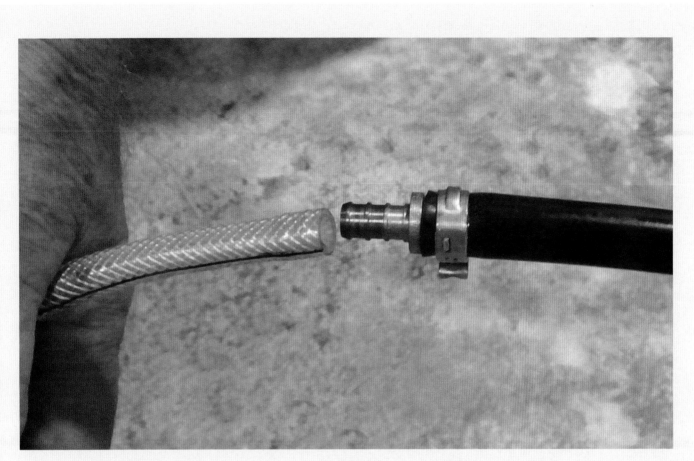

Jim's compost brewing system connects the copper piping and churning apparatus to the pump outside of the bucket.

2. The top section of copper piping forms a square to hold the mesh bag or nylon sock, using plastic clips as an optional and supplemental form of containment. A mesh bag with handle, made to fit and extended about half way down the bucket, works well with this design.

3. A pipe runs downward alongside the edge of the bucket to connect to an outlet on each side of the bucket (see next page). Part of this set up includes piping attached to the upper part of the bucket that drapes over its side.

4. The churner at the bottom of the bucket features opposite directional ends that aid in making a strong current during the 8-24 hour brewing process. These ends also come with modified holes for air injection.

Do-It-Yourself Steps to Brewing Compost Tea *(continued)*

BEARD'S BREWER (continued)

Opposite directional heads are at the end of Jim's compost brewing system.

This view of Jim's compost brewing system awaits the arrival of a sock or a net filled with worm castings to brew natural plant nutrition.

- Some of the items Jim uses to make this device also include 4 caps, 6 elbows, 5 Ts, a $^1/_2$-inch hose adapter, and 2 capped directional ends with manufactured holes for air injection. Again, custom fit these alterations to preference.

Beard's Behind-the-Blueprint Tip:

Harvard University is a pioneer innovator in compost tea production and application. Its Energy & Facilities Organic Maintenance Program is full of additional resources, including compost tea brewers of large scale proportions.

*To learn more, visit **www.energyandfacilities. harvard.edu.***

Beard's Behind-the-Blueprint Tip:

Jim suggests checking out the line of organic stuff at IntelliGROWTH in Appleton, Wisconsin. Some of what you'll find there complements subject matter in this book, and you can also learn about all the hubbub surrounding worm castings as one of the best sources of organic compost.

*Visit **www.peatys.com** and tell the good folks there that Jim Beard sent you on behalf of Growing People.*

4

This & That, Here & There

Observe growing communities, enjoy a few additional resources, meet us on paper, tip your hat to our sources, and stay in touch!

11 Depictions of Discovery

Lives are changing for the better all around us if we stop long enough to smell the flowers.

Enjoy this pictorial tour of growing people and places, along with some visuals that may help you enhance a garden space or two.

Larry London, Executive Chef, ThedaCare

Jim Beard and his students developed a sustainable gem for our health care community with an organic growing system of various raised beds and straw bales at Appleton Medical Center.

I have sampled a lot of greens in my career, and without a doubt, his straw bale garden produced the best parsley I have ever tasted.

— Larry London, Executive Chef, ThedaCare

People growers Bill Henry and Jim Beard work with their friend, Bill Shinkan (ladder), on a new structure for the Outagamie County Insane Asylum Cemetery. Keep your eye on this warmhearted project to help memorialize the resting souls of yesteryear. [31]

Healthy greens start with a little TLC as micros in the Hydroponics Lab at Fox Valley Technical College, where a lot of people growing takes place in both students and community members.

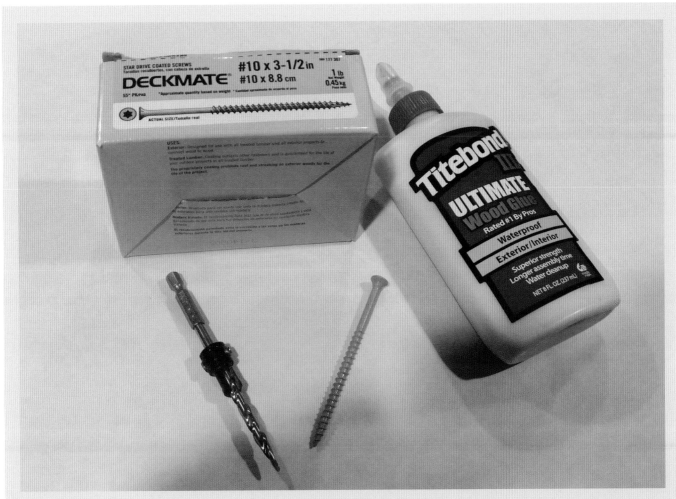

Your bread-and-butter necessities for all things construction in this book

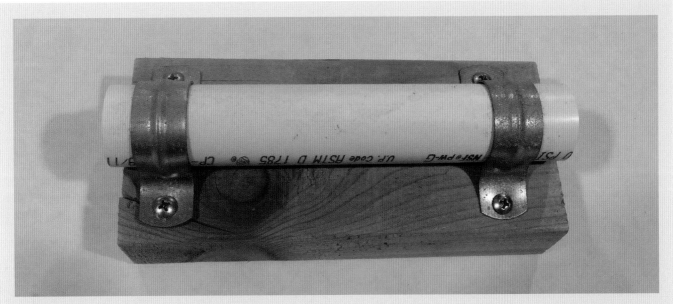

One-inch PVC piping is anchored and then attached vertically to the sides of traditional raised beds to serve as hoop insertion stanchions.

Jim Beard led the development of the Lowe's Foundation Sustainable Greenhouse at Fox Valley Technical College. [32]

The Hartling Family Rose Garden between entrances 3 and 4 at Fox Valley Technical College, conceptualized by Jim Beard, was highlighted in *USA Today*. (33)

Moments of respite are found at every turn in the Hartling Family Rose Garden. [34]

Irrigation System Illustrations

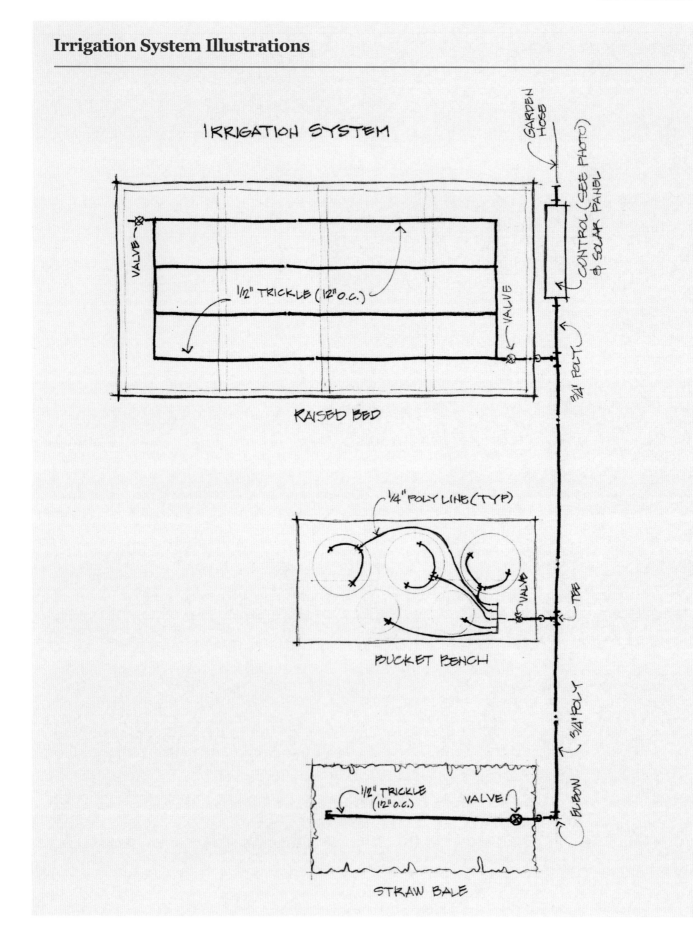

IRRIGATION SYSTEM

RAISED BED

BUCKET BENCH

STRAW BALE

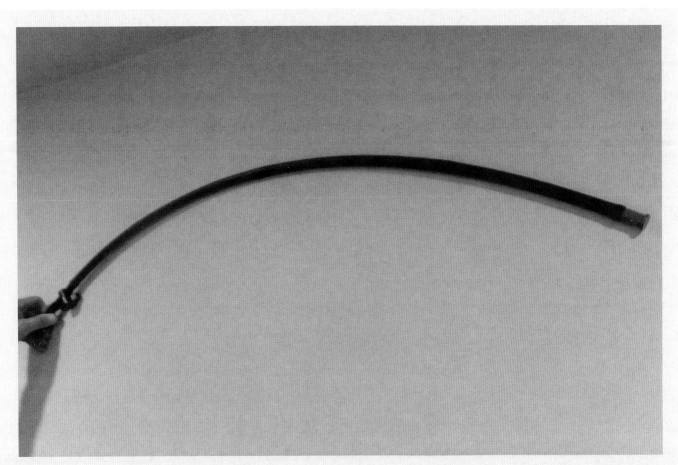

Netafim® trickle pipe for straw bales with a plug on one end and a valve on the other feeds a water line.

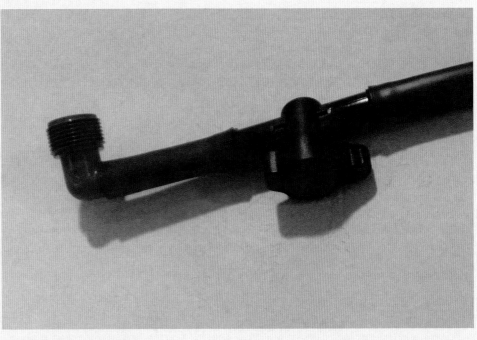

On/off valve shown here

Irrigation System Illustrations *(continued)*

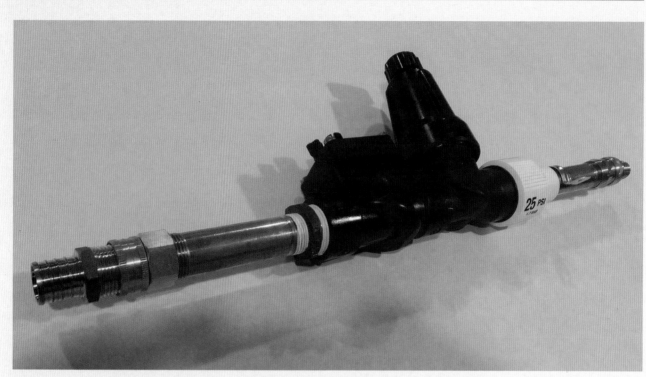

The main control valve of a consumer-style irrigation system connects to a standard garden hose on the left and a discharge device on the right to distribute water to straw bales and both traditional and bucket bench raised beds.

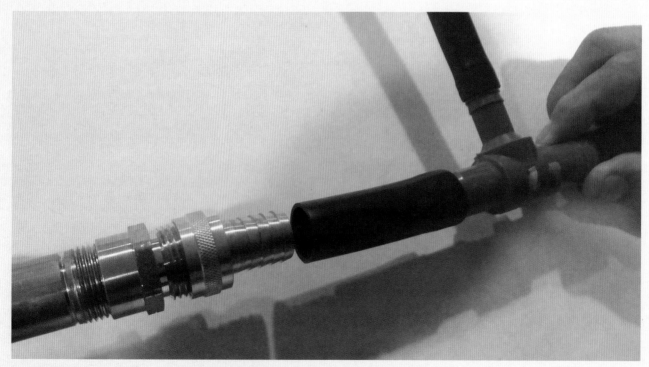

A discharge device of choice connects to the right end of the main control valve of a consumer-style irrigation system.

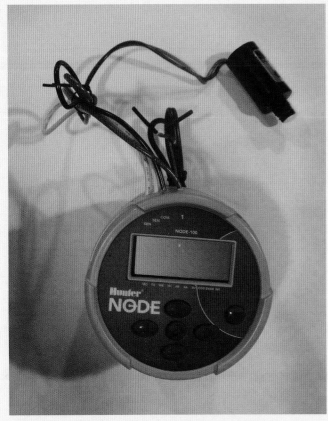

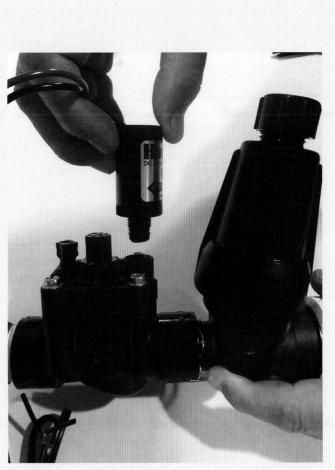

A standard controller programs water distribution for a consumer-style irrigation system without the need of an electrical connection.

The controller connects to the top of the main control valve.

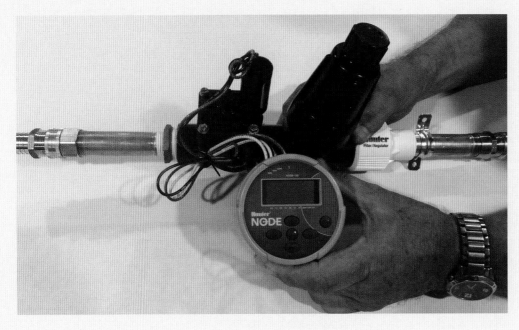

The controller and main control valve are now connected.

Irrigation System Illustrations *(continued)*

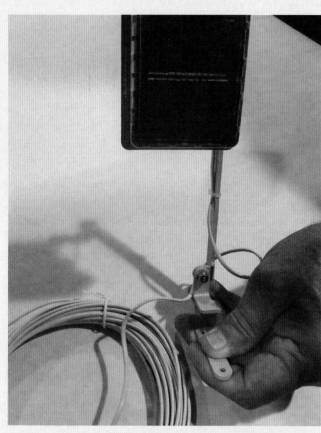

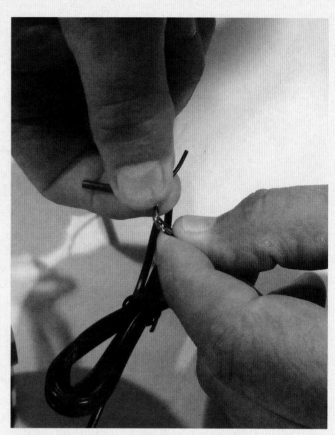

A small solar panel is ideal for generating power to the organic growing systems highlighted in this book.

A little wiring (by following manufacturer's instructions) connects the solar panel to the main control valve.

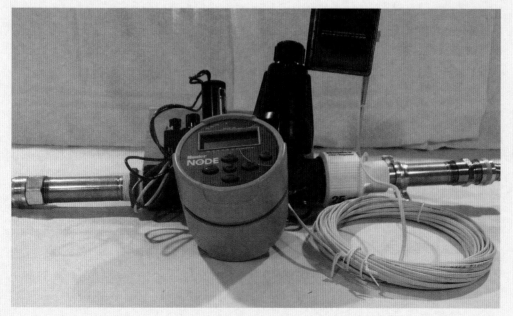

A solar-style consumer irrigation system optimizes the watering of your organic gardens.

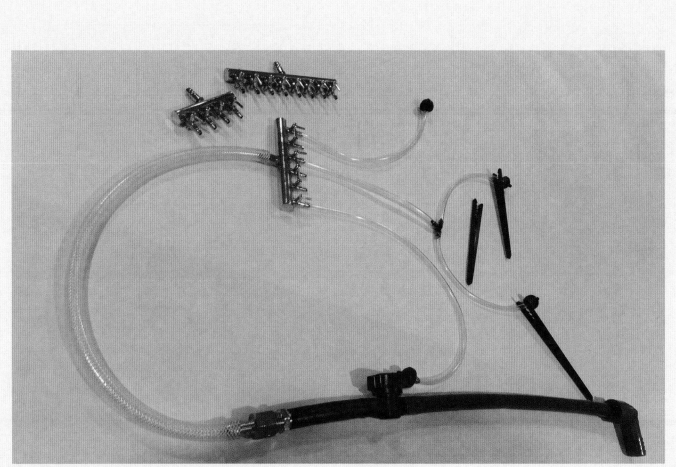

Presented here are the basic items needed for watering a raised bucket bench by way of a solar-style consumer irrigation system.

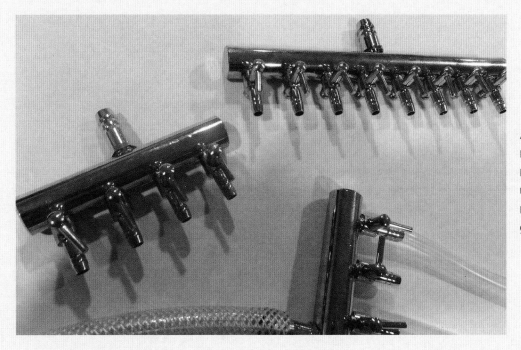

A close-up look at metal port-style manifold options used to water raised bucket bench gardens

Irrigation System Illustrations *(continued)*

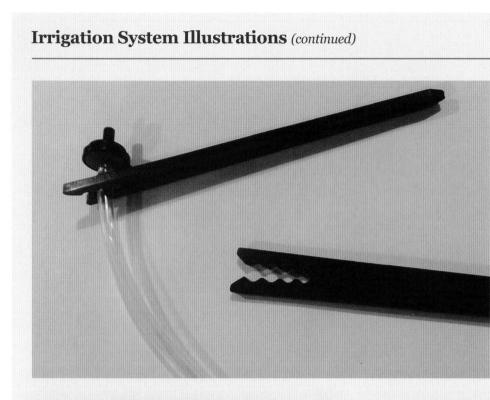

A quarter-inch polyethylene tube and plastic holders work together to keep emitters in place.

A highway of watering for your raised bucket bench gardens

A top-side view of the solar-style consumer irrigation system and raised bucket bed garden, together

The entrance point of a consumer-style irrigation system into a traditional raised bed

A solar panel for the type of growing described in this book is easily mountable for an aesthetic blend into a garden space.

If you didn't have a chance to visit the Wisconsin State Fair this year, then you missed the Straw Bale Cage designed and built by the Fox Valley Technical College Horticulture program and displayed in the WE Energies Park.

— Excerpt appeared in the September 2015 newsletter of the Wisconsin Landscape Contractors Association

Once students realize they don't know everything, then you're in a position to teach them anything. I've been there and still am as a student of life.

There are people who have just enough knowledge to get themselves in trouble when it comes to a project, but not enough knowledge to get out of it.

— Jim Beard

Closing Thoughts: Growing People has Gone Global

While writing this book I realized that Jim Beard's growing of people comes without borders. I learned about an international student from Central America that Jim, along with Agriculture program instructor Randy Tenpas, took under their wing about a year ago. The young man was attending Fox Valley Technical College to study plants and soil conditions. He plans to take that knowledge back to his homeland to improve lives in a third-world nation. The college empowers a large number of international students each year in specialized training.

In the case with Jim and Randy, the young man wanted to do anything and everything around the clock to consume as much knowledge outside of the classroom as well. He was fascinated by Jim and Randy's relationships with people and wanted to learn how to develop lifelong friendships.

Whenever and wherever there was something going on around the Service Motor Company Agriculture Center at Fox Valley Technical College, this student would be there—hanging out with other students. He even showed up at the college here and there during winter to lend a hand shoveling snow at 5:00 a.m. Central America and snow? We bet that will make for a good story back home.

With some guidance, the student landed a seasonal job working in a garden center for a local landscaper. He would water plants, trim bushes, and perform other light miscellaneous tasks.

One day Jim saw the student at work after about a month of working for the landscaping firm. He asked the young man how the job was going. He proudly replied with a grin wider than the Pacific, "I get to wear a shirt with my company's name on it."

It's like this young man won the lottery. How do you measure growing people?

Takeaways

Some people have already asked me what it was like to write this book with Jim. I learned three invaluable takeaways from this experience:

1. A 2 by 4 is not really 2 by 4.
2. Technical knowledge and the art of narrative can enjoy a solid partnership… the laughs, stories, and cups of coffee together were priceless.
3. If there were more "Jim Beards" in this world, our society would be a better place.

People who shine from within do not need a spotlight.

Author Profiles

Jim Beard, ASLA, AOLCP

Jim has more than 40 years of both industry experience and as an instructor. His work in the landscape design and construction field included the likes of serving as director of facilities for St. Norbert College and as an architect for Boldt, with additional industry experience in project management. Prior to his professional work, Jim served nearly four years in the United States Army—which included a tour of duty in Vietnam.

Certified in Organic Land Care from the Northeast Organic Farming Association and as a state-level Certified Landscape Architect, Jim's green thumb roots are rich in history. In the mid-1970s, he led volunteers in the implementation of organic play pockets for children, families, and schools in Green Bay. The effort grew into a model for volunteers to follow in other regions as well. Play pockets were also put in communities around northern Illinois and in the Upper Peninsula of Michigan—about 190 in all, covering three states when the project was said and done in the early 1980s. Jim earned three awards as a result of the play pocket movement, including a State Senate Proclamation and the 1977 Wisconsin Jaycee's Outstanding Young Man award.

Jim has directed the time and talents of volunteers on several other notable landscape construction projects and green makeovers as lead Horticulture instructor at Fox Valley Technical College (FVTC). A 9/11 Memorial in Greenville, the Hartling Family Rose Garden, a series of organic gardens for ThedaCare, and the Green Roof Rest Station—recognized as a Gold Medal structure from the Wisconsin Landscape Contractors Association, are just a few of the marks he and his students have made on others.

The winner of the 2008 H. Victor Baldi Excellence in Instruction award at FVTC, Jim's passion for education is found in his ongoing commitment to high-tech learning resources at FVTC. He was the brainchild behind the college's development of the Lowe's Foundation Sustainable Greenhouse, Hydroponics Lab, and the Ron Amos Horticulture Tissue Lab (which was made possible by the generosity of Evergreen Nursery Company, Inc. and Boldt).

Today, Jim serves as an Emeritus Member of the American Society of Landscape Architects while continuing to teach as lead instructor in the Horticulture Technician program at FVTC. He enjoys giving a wide range of lectures across the state and Midwest, particularly on his new growing systems: Beds, Bales, Buckets, and Brews.

Christopher Jossart, MA

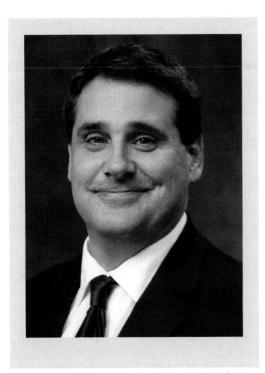

Chris is a public relations management professional with 22 years of experience in the non-profit, corporate, and education fields. His 14 years of instructional experience in higher education grew into a new venture as a personal branding trainer for both individuals and corporations in 2014. The culinary arts, human services, information technology, horticulture, and educational industries have all benefitted thus far from Chris' expertise in personal brand development.

In addition, Chris is an author, award-winning editor in higher education for a college magazine, and writer with international bylines, in addition to ghostwriting nationally-published content for doctorate-level professionals. His first book, *The Human Search Engine: It's what you think you know about a job search that keeps you unemployed*, has been adopted as a textbook in accredited higher education, used by Division 1 collegiate athletes as a career planning guide, and implemented as supplemental learning material for college students in life skills studies. The book, which gained national recognition as a job search model on behalf of the 103rd United States Congress, is now a second edition based on demand. It can be found at www.hsethebook.com.

As a persuasive writer, Chris has written seven winning nominations for individuals and organizations related to both community recognition events and initiatives in business and industry. These ventures gained media attention, and in some cases, financial support for non-profit organizations. In 2004, Chris also wrote curriculum for a program designed to teach elementary-aged youth about personal safety; the learning module received both corporate sponsorship and praise from the National Center for Missing & Exploited Children.

Chris' leadership in public relations was instrumental in Fox Valley Technical College's (FVTC) passage of a $66.5 million public referendum in 2012. His work for the college has appeared in *USA Today, The Wall Street Journal, United States Department of Labor Newsletter, the Community College Times, and Christian Science Monitor*, to name a few. Earlier in his career, Chris presented and consulted at state and national conferences on volunteer recruitment and management. Most recently, he gave the keynote address at FVTC's 2015 HSED/GED Graduation Ceremony.

Chris holds a Master of Arts degree in Managerial Communications and a Provisional Teaching Certificate from the Wisconsin Technical College System.

Inquiries

Lectures, consultation, general questions about content in the book:

chris@mypageturner.com

Acknowledgments

1. Design of front cover by Cara Jakubiec

2-4. Photos courtesy of Fox Valley Technical College

5. Design of back cover by Cara Jakubiec

6. Photo courtesy of Gary Gawinski

7. Photo courtesy of a student at Fox Valley Technical College as an anonymous contributor

8. X-factor instruction is a service of Passion Branding, a Registered Trademark of Chris & Kim Jossart, Appleton, Wisconsin, as a two-part training program series.

9. Passion Building is a Registered Trademark of Chris & Kim Jossart, Appleton, Wisconsin, as a two-part training program series.

10-22. Photos courtesy of Fox Valley Technical College

23. Photo courtesy of Gary Gawinski

24. Photo courtesy of Fox Valley Technical College

25-29. Photos courtesy of Steve Finley

30. Photo courtesy of Fox Valley Technical College

31. Photo courtesy of Steve Finley

32-34. Photos courtesy of Fox Valley Technical College

- Photo on Welcome page of Ms. Melinda Myers courtesy of Mark Avery

- Photo of Jim Beard in Author Profiles chapter courtesy of Fox Valley Technical College

- Photo of Christopher Jossart in Author Profiles chapter courtesy of Adam Shea Photography